Collaborative Web Search

Who, What, Where, When, and Why

Collaborative Web Search: Who, What, Where, When, and Why

Meredith Ringel Morris and Jaime Teevan

ISBN:978-3-031-01142-9   paperback
ISBN: 978-3-031-02270-8   ebook

DOI 10.1007/978-3-031-02270-8

A Publication in the Springer series
SYNTHESIS LECTURES ON INFORMATION CONCEPTS, RETRIEVAL, AND SERVICES

Lecture #14
Series Editor: Gary Marchionini, *University North Carolina, Chapel Hill*
Series ISSN
Synthesis Lectures on Information Concepts, Retrieval, and Services
Print 1947-945X   Electronic 1947-9468

Synthesis Lectures on Information Concepts, Retrieval, and Services

Collaborative Web Search

Who, What, Where, When, and Why

Meredith Ringel Morris and Jaime Teevan
Microsoft Research

SYNTHESIS LECTURES ON INFORMATION CONCEPTS, RETRIEVAL, AND SERVICES #14

ABSTRACT

Today, Web search is treated as a solitary experience. Web browsers and search engines are typically designed to support a single user, working alone. However, collaboration on information-seeking tasks is actually commonplace. Students work together to complete homework assignments, friends seek information about joint entertainment opportunities, family members jointly plan vacation travel, and colleagues jointly conduct research for their projects. As improved networking technologies and the rise of social media simplify the process of remote collaboration, and large, novel display form-factors simplify the process of co-located group work, researchers have begun to explore ways to facilitate collaboration on search tasks.

This lecture investigates the *who*, *what*, *where*, *when* and *why* of collaborative search, and gives insight in *how* emerging solutions can address collaborators' needs.

KEYWORDS

Web search, collaborative search, social search, collaborative information retrieval, HCI, CSCW, social computing

Contents

Acknowledgments

We would like to thank our colleagues and interns from Microsoft whose efforts have contributed to our exploration of collaborative search. In particular, we would like to acknowledge Saleema Amershi, Steve Bush, Susan Dumais, Danyel Fisher, Björn Hartmann, Eric Horvitz, Petra Isenberg, Jarrod Lombardo, Katrina Panovich, Sharoda Paul, and Daniel Wigdor.

Meredith Ringel Morris and Jaime Teevan
December 2009

Credits

Figures 2.1 and 2.2,
Pickens, J., Golovchinsky, G., Shah, C., Qvarfordt, P. and Back, M. (2008) Algorithmic Mediation for Collaborative Exploratory Search. *Proceedings of SIGIR 2008*, 315-322. Copyright © 2008 Association for Computing Machinery. Reprinted by permission. DOI: 10.1145/1390334.1390389

Figure 2.3,
Morris, M.R., Teevan, J., and Bush, S. (2008) Enhancing Collaborative Web Search with Personalization: Groupization, Smart Splitting, and Group Hit-Highlighting. *Proceedings of CSCW 2008*, 481-484. Copyright © 2008 Association for Computing Machinery. DOI: 10.1145/1460563.1460640

Figure 2.4,
Teevan, J., Morris, M.R., and Bush, S. (2009b) Discovering and Using Groups to Improve Personalized Search. *Proceedings of WSDM 2009*, 15-24. Copyright © 2009 Association for Computing Machinery. DOI: 10.1145/1498759.1498786

Figure 3.2,
Paul, S. A. and Morris, M.R. (2009) CoSense: Enhancing Sensemaking for Collaborative Web Search. *Proceedings of CHI 2009*, 1771-1780. Copyright © 2009 Association for Computing Machinery.

Figure 4.1,
Smyth, B., Briggs, P., Coyle, M., and O'Mahoney, M. (2009) Google Shared: A Case Study in Social Search. *Proceedings of UMAP 2009*. © *2009 Springer*. With kind permission of Springer Science+Business Media. DOI: 10.1007/s00530-006-0064-7

Figure 4.2,
Romano, N., Nunamaker, J., Roussinov, D., and Chen, H. (1999) Collaborative Information Retrieval Environment: Integration of Information Retrieval with Group Support Systems. *Proceedings of the Hawaii International Conference on System Sciences*, 1999. © IEEE 1999, DOI: 10.1109/HICSS.1999.772729 Used with permission.

Figure 4.3,
Morris, M.R., Teevan, J., and Bush, S. (2008) Enhancing Collaborative Web Search with Personalization: Groupization, Smart Splitting, and Group Hit-Highlighting. *Proceedings of CSCW 2008*, 481-484.

Figure 4.15,
Morris, M.R., Fisher, D., and Wigdor, D. (2010a) Search on Surfaces: Exploring the Potential of Interactive Tabletops for Collaborative Search Tasks. *Information Processing and Management*, in press. Copyright © 2009 Elsevier Ltd. DOI: 10.1016/j.ipm2009.10.004

Figure 4.16,
Tuddenham, P., Davies, I., and Robinson, P. (2009) WebSurface: An Interface for Colocated Collaborative Information Gathering. *Proceedings of Tabletop 2009*, 201-208. Copyright © 2009 Association for Computing Machinery.

Figures 4.18-4.20,
Amershi,S.and Morris,M.R. (2008) CoSearch: A System for Co-located Collaborative Web Search. *Proceedings of CHI 2008*, 1647-1656. Copyright © 2008 Association for Computing Machinery DOI: 10.1145/1357054.1357311

Figure 4.25,
Wiltse, H., and Nichols, J. (2009) PlayByPlay: Collaborative Web Browsing for Desktop and Mobile Devices. *Proceedings of CHI 2009*, 1781-1790. Copyright © 2009 Association for Computing Machinery. Reprinted by permission. DOI: 10.1145/1518701.1518975

Figure 5.1 and 5.2,
Morris, M.R. and Horvitz, E. (2007a) S^3: Storable, Shareable Search. *Proceedings of Interact 2007*, 120–123. Copyright © 2007 Association for Computing Machinery.

Figures 5.4-5.7,
Paul, S. A. and Morris, M.R. (2009) CoSense: Enhancing Sensemaking for Collaborative Web Search. *Proceedings of CHI 2009*, 1771-1780. Copyright © 2009 Association for Computing Machinery.

CHAPTER 1

Introduction

Web search has become one of the prominent information behaviors of the new millennium (Fallows, D., 2008). *Web search* refers not only to the process of entering keywords into a search engine site, but it also includes a related ecology of online information-seeking activities, such as browsing to specific URLs, making sense of found content, iteratively revising a query, and disseminating results. Web searches may be accomplished with a single query, or they may span multiple work sessions. For example, exploratory search tasks (White et al., 2006; White and Roth, 2009) can potentially last days, months, or even longer.

Traditionally, the tools that facilitate Web search have been designed for solitary use. Web search engines, for example, are designed for a single person to enter a few keywords related to what they are looking for, and then sift individually through a list of the results the search engine returns. More generally, when people search for information online, they typically use Web search engines or other sites merely as starting-off points to orienteer to an information target (Teevan et al., 2004), but even such broader considerations of the use of Web browsers and link following for information seeking are primarily studied as and designed for the single user scenario.

Despite Web search's focus on the individual user, there are many situations in which people choose to collaborate on a shared search task. For example, students may need to jointly research a group homework assignment, family members might seek information about a loved one's medical condition, or friends might plan vacation travel together (Morris, M.R., 2008). The process of more than one person searching in collaboration with others for a shared goal is called *collaborative search*.

When groups of people searching with a shared goal are able to effectively collaborate on Web search tasks, they can enjoy several advantages over solo searching, such as increased coverage of the relevant information space, higher confidence in the quality of their findings, and greater productivity due to a reduction in unnecessary redundant work (Morris, M.R., 2007). Tools designed to support collaboration as a first-class aspect of Web search have the potential to offer substantial benefits over status quo tools.

However, a one-size-fits-all solution to collaborative search seems unlikely. The term "collaboration" encompasses a variety of work configurations that vary along several dimensions, such as *who* comprises the collaborative group and how they relate to each other (symmetric or asymmetric), *what* aspects of the search they need to collaborate on (the process or the product), *where* the collaborators are located (co-located or remote), *when* the collaboration occurs (synchronously or asynchronously), or *why* the group has been formed (explicitly or implicitly). In this lecture, we review the body of work done to understand the needs for each of these work styles and to design and evaluate collaborative search systems for each scenario.

1.1   COLLABORATIVE SEARCH IN CONTEXT

Collaborative search is part of the broader emerging phenomenon called *social search*. Social search refers broadly to the process of finding information online with the assistance of social resources. For example, most commercial search engines use some social resources to improve the search experience. The results other searchers have clicked (Joachims, T., 2002) and the links other people make between information resources (Kleinberg, J., 1999) are used in ranking Web search results, and past group query behavior is used to suggest relevant related search keywords (Cao et al., 2008) or even replace the user's existing query (Jones et al., 2006).

All Web content is to some degree social in nature, being primarily created and shared by people other than the person consuming the content. Although social search is typically not used to refer to the use of Web content in general, it can refer to searches conducted over existing databases of content created for social purposes, such as the collection of public Twitter posts http://twitter.com/, or an archive of questions and answers, such as in the Answer Garden system (Ackerman and Malone, 1990). Search over databases of socially-generated content, collaborative filtering, and other similar mechanisms represent *implicitly social* activities. Users of such systems are not actively attempting to assist each other in their search efforts, and they may not even be aware that their actions have influenced others' search outcomes.

However, other people often explicitly aid an individual's search task in many steps of the search process. In a 2008 survey, Wells and Rainie (2008) found that people used a mixture of internet searching and social resources (i.e., phone calls or face-to-face meetings) in order to answer many types of questions. Some researchers have proposed formal models to describe the interplay of online information seeking with the use of social resources. For example, Pirolli, P. (2009) developed a model of social information foraging, and Evans and Chi (2008) described the various stages in the search process when users engaged with other people. Some researchers have built special tools to integrate explicit social information with search engine use, such as HeyStaks (Smyth et al., 2009), a browser plug-in that enables users to mark search results as relevant; these results are then boosted in the rankings of socially connected users who do searches on similar topics.

In all of the above examples of social search, social information is used, either implicitly or explicitly, to improve what is primarily an individual user's search experience. *Collaborative search*, which we focus on in this lecture, is the subset of social search where more than one user share an information need, and they actively work together to fulfill that need. Although collaborative search is our main focus, we occasionally refer to findings from the broader social search literature when such findings can inform the design of more explicitly collaborative systems.

1.2   SCENARIO: COLLABORATION TODAY

To aid in our discussion of collaborative search, we consider a scenario representing collaborative search as it occurs today. The scenario occurs shortly after Martha's breathing difficulties were diagnosed by her doctor as asthma. Immediately after the diagnosis, Martha headed back to her office and did a bit of research during her lunch break. She wanted to learn more about the causes of adult-onset asthma and to investigate the treatments her doctor had prescribed. Her goal was to learn whether less expensive medications, or perhaps even simple lifestyle changes, might improve her condition.

Martha found some websites listing possible causes of asthma, and she noticed that one possible cause is environmental irritants. Via a new search and some link-following, she found a list of common environmental irritants that may cause respiratory disorders, and she printed it out so that she could show it to her husband.

When she arrived home from work that evening, she went over the printed pages with her husband, George, and they discussed which irritants might be present in their home. Martha and George were unsure how to check whether their house contained the types of molds included on the irritant list, so they turned on their home computer to investigate further. George sat at the keyboard and Martha stood behind him, looking over his shoulder.

George wanted to re-find the website with the irritant list Martha had printed, hoping they might be able to click through from that site to learn more details about household molds. Martha tried to remember the URL for the site, but could not. Instead, she tried to re-create the original path she used to find it, suggesting that George try typing "asthma causes" into a search engine. Pointing at the screen, Martha told George that the fourth link looked familiar, but George decided instead to click on the second link since its snippet description sounded similar to the text on the printed page. The page did not match, so George went back to the results list, this time following Martha's suggestion and finding the desired irritant list. On that page, George found a link describing molds in more detail and clicked it. As he read about identifying household molds, he scrolled quickly through the page, and Martha was unable to keep up with his reading speed. Frustrated, she left George to continue searching on his own and called her sister, Beth, to discuss her diagnosis.

After speaking to Martha, Beth wanted to learn more about her sister's condition, so she performed a Web search about common causes of adult-onset asthma. She copied and pasted the links she found into an email, and she sent them to Martha. The next day, Martha checked her email and found the list of links from Beth. Unfortunately, the links were to the sites listing common household irritants, which Martha had already found; Beth had unknowingly duplicated Martha's own research.

Martha also had an email from George, reminding her to ask her colleague, Jim, what mold-inspection company he used on his home last year, since George's research from the night before determined that they needed to hire a professional to clear their house of potential respiratory irritants, and Martha recalled that Jim recently had his house checked for similar issues. Prompted by the email, Martha stopped by Jim's office to ask him what firm he selected to inspect his home for mold last year. Although Jim had invested a great deal of effort into researching the pros and cons of different inspection companies, comparing the services, pricing, and reputation of several local businesses, he did not explicitly save this content, and he could not easily share it with Martha.

So Martha returned to her office and began the process of identifying mold-cleaning companies on her own. After finding one that seemed reasonably priced, she sent an instant message to her husband with a link to the company's site, and she asked him if the company looked good to him. George replied to Martha's IM, asking whether she had remembered to check the reputation of the company on a local business review site. Martha replied to George, suggesting a division of labor so that they would not duplicate each other's efforts the way she and Beth had – she would send George a list of local mold-cleaning companies, and George could be responsible for finding reputation information for each company, while she would find pricing information. At the end of the work day, the two shared and discussed their findings at home, and, they eventually, decided on a company to call.

Although Martha's story is fictional, her attempts to collaborate with George, Beth, and Jim illustrate the challenges faced by users of today's status quo search technologies and the cumbersome work-arounds many employ (Morris, M.R., 2008; Amershi and Morris, 2008). The collaborative search systems we discuss in this lecture attempt to improve many aspects of this process. In the conclusion of this lecture, we revisit Martha's scenario in light of recent advances in collaborative searching, to see how newly-proposed technologies might support sharing her information-finding workload in the manner she desires.

1.3   OVERVIEW OF LECTURE

In the upcoming discussion, we will answer the following questions: *Who* are the people who engage in collaborative searches, and what is the nature of the relationships among these collaborators? *What* type of collaborative search tasks do people engage in, and what phases of these tasks provide opportunities for collaboration? *Where* are collaborators located – in the same location, or in different locations? *When* does the collaboration take place – do group members work simultaneously, or at different times? *Why* was the group formed – based on a shared topical interest, as the result of an existing social connection, or serendipitously, based on group members' implicit characteristics?

1.3.1   WHO?

We begin with a discussion of the categories of people who search collaboratively. For example, family members like Martha, George, and Beth, often collaborate on searches. Students are another common group of collaborators, working together on class assignments. We also look at the makeup of groups, discussing typical group size and the roles group members assume. Additionally, we examine common relationships among collaborators, such as whether they take on symmetric asymmetric roles in the search task. Understanding more about the people and groups who perform collaborative searches can allow system designers to better target the solutions they build.

1.3.2   WHAT?

We then look at what people's tasks are when they search collaboratively. Many tasks in both professional and casual settings can benefit from the ability to jointly search the Web with others, and such situations appear to be commonplace. We explore whether people need or want to collaborate on certain tasks when searching the Web. We also look at what strategies people currently employ to collaborate using current search interfaces not explicitly designed to support collaborative search.

We further break down common search strategies to consider more specifically what aspects of these tasks may benefit from collaboration. For example, collaboration can occur over the process of searching or over the products of a search. When Martha suggests query terms to George as they search together to learn more about common irritants, they are collaborating on the process of search. And when Beth shares the list of links she finds with Martha, she is collaborating over the product of her search. We examine specific search tactics that offer collaboration opportunities in greater detail, considering work from the library sciences as well as the digital domain to identify common patterns.

1.3.3   WHERE?

Another important dimension of collaborative search is where the participants are located relative to the other collaborators. The members of the group may or may not be physically located in the same location and may or may not be using the same machine. In our scenario, Martha and George searched together on the same machine, while Martha and Beth collaborated remotely on separate machines.

When collaborators are not physically located in the same place, we refer to their interaction as *remote collaboration*. We investigate the affordances important for supporting remote collaborative searches, such as support for awareness and division of labor among participants, and we examine the SearchTogether system (Morris and Horvitz, 2007b) as an in-depth example.

Some systems designed to support collaborative search have focused on *co-located collaboration*, when all group members are physically co-present. We discuss the needs of co-located collaborators, and explore how different device arrangements afford distinct design opportunities. For example, CoSearch (Amershi and Morris, 2008) facilitates co-located collaborative search by providing a private input device (a mobile phone) for each group member, whereas WeSearch (Morris et al., 2010b) uses a single, shared multi-touch display.

1.3.4   WHEN?

Another interesting dimension of collaborative search is when the collaboration occurs. Collaborative search activities can occur synchronously, with collaborators working simultaneously to find what they are looking for, or asynchronously, with collaborators working individually in support of a shared search goal.

Most current commercial search tools are better suited to asynchronous, rather than synchronous, collaboration. Martha's sister Beth, for example, researched her sister's recently diagnosed asthma on a Web search engine while Martha did other things, and emailed a list of interesting links to Martha for further exploration at a different time. Systems designed to support asynchronous collaboration typically do so by creating a persistent representation of Web investigations that facilitates suspension and resumption of search tasks; we explore the S^3 system (Morris and Horvitz, 2007a) as an in-depth example of this approach.

As an example of synchronous collaborative search, a group of coworkers may gather around a computer to research a topic of interest, with one person controlling the mouse and keyboard and the others offering comments and suggestions, as was done by Martha and George during their search for common asthma irritants. Many systems have been designed to support synchronous collaborative search within specialized domains or with specialized devices (e.g., TeamSearch (Morris et al., 2006), C-TORI (Hoppe and Zhao, 1994), and MUSE (Krishnappa, R., 2005)). Other systems that support synchronous collaborative search are more general, such as SearchTogether (Morris and Horvitz, 2007b). The different temporal configurations impact the options collaboration tools should offer to searchers. Studies of the CoSense system (Paul and Morris, 2009), during both asynchronous and synchronous collaborative search scenarios, have found that these two collaboration styles benefit from different types of sensemaking support.

1.3.5   WHY?

Research can also give us insight into why people work with the group members they do during collaborative search activities. We begin this chapter by discussing how people are brought together because of a shared interest in a common topic. For examples, Martha's asthma diagnosis makes the topic of interest to her family members, and it inspires the group to work together to learn more about the disease. Tools like question-answering systems (e.g., Ackerman and Malone (1990)) and expertise-finding systems (e.g., Bernstein et al. (2009)) help bring together people with shared interests.

But people also collaborate during search for social reasons. Beth may help her sister find information about her asthma not just because Beth is interested in learning more about asthma, but also because it helps bring her closer to her sister, makes her feel good about herself, or even makes it more likely that Martha will help her in the future with some task that interests her. Systems can support the social aspects of collaborative search by providing awareness for all group members of how individuals contribute to the shared goal, much as is done on Q&A websites (Raban and Harper, 2008).

Although we focus in this lecture on intentional collaborations, there are many examples where people implicitly collaborate with others on search tasks. For example, the links people click (Joachims, T., 2002) and the queries people issue (Kleinberg, J., 1999) feed back into many commercial search systems to improve the experience of future people searching on the same topic. Understanding when implicit groups stand to benefit from collaborative interventions provides opportunities for systems to suggest serendipitous group formation, creating the opportunity for implicit collaborations to transform into explicit ones.

In the following chapters, we dive more deeply into the *who, what, where, when,* and *why* of collaborative search. It is our hope that in doing so, we give insight into *how* emerging solutions might best address collaborators' future needs.

CHAPTER 2

Who?

This chapter paints a picture of the people who engage in collaborative search activities. One important aspect of this involves understanding the properties of specific user groups. Certain populations, such as students and families, are particularly likely to collaborate on search activities. But it is also important to understand how collaborative groups are composed. Group members do not always all assume the same role, but rather sometimes partition the work along several common axes. Understanding group members' roles and relationships to one another in the real world helps provide insight into how collaborative search systems might best support them.

2.1 SPECIFIC POPULATIONS

Researchers have identified several specific user populations who engage in collaborative search activities, including library patrons, students, information workers, and families. Because libraries have existed as information sources much longer than the World Wide Web, one of the more commonly studied population of collaborative searchers is patrons of libraries. In these instances, the person with the information need often arrives at the library with an individual search goal and enlists one or more other experts to collaborate with them in satisfying this goal. Traditionally, this service has been provided in person at libraries by reference librarians (Taylor, R., 1968). Similar capabilities are now also available digitally through services such as Question Point (http://www.oclc.org/questionpoint). Question Point provides real-time online access to librarians embedded within library webpages or other Web portals, and communication is supported via chat and cooperative browsing tools.

Some populations are particularly likely to engage in collaborative search at a library. Amershi and Morris (2008) found that senior citizens and recent immigrants frequently engage in collaborative searches using library computers, mainly because they are unfamiliar with the technology. These searches are typically mediated by library staff or more skilled family members. Library staff are trained to avoid taking over input devices while collaboratively searching so that their collaborators can become comfortable with the technology. Instead, staff members typically guide the search by making query suggestions (verbally or on paper) or navigation suggestions (by manually pointing).

Students of all ages also often collaborate in libraries and classrooms as part of in-class activities or homework assignments. Large et al. (2002) reported that elementary school students often collaborate on information seeking tasks, due both to group-learning pedagogies and to resource constraints. Amershi and Morris' interviews with librarians and teachers revealed that collaboration on

Web search was also common among middle- and high-school aged students (Amershi and Morris, 2008); for example, one librarian in their study noted that collaboration seemed to be a common trend among teenagers, whom she observed to always gather in groups around the library's Internet terminals except when checking their email. Twidale et al. (1997) found that university students frequently worked together on information-seeking tasks in the college library, engaging in social activities such as offering advice to fellow library users or asking a neighboring computer user how they accomplished something.

Information workers are another group with collaborative information seeking needs. Fidel et al. (2000) found that office workers frequently collaborated when retrieving information from traditional sources, such as books. Morris, M.R. (2008) found that information workers engaged in a variety of collaborative behaviors when conducting Web searches. Evans and Chi (2008) survey of Mechanical Turk users about social search interactions also revealed that many information workers in fields such as education, finance, healthcare, and government engaged with others while searching.

In addition to library patrons, students, and information workers, families are another type of group that also often have shared information needs, and they collaborate on satisfying those needs. An example of this is Martha's collaborations with her husband George and sister Beth to learn more about her asthma diagnosis. When users participated in a diary study of collaborative searches performed either at work or at home (Amershi and Morris, 2009), participants reported engaging in several family-oriented collaborative searches, such as planning weekend activities or purchasing theatre tickets. Family groups trying the WeSearch system (Morris et al., 2010b) engaged in tasks such as planning upcoming vacations and shopping for a new home computer. A survey study of information workers' collaborative search habits (Morris, M.R., 2008), though not focused on at-home activities, nonetheless found that respondents provided examples of familial collaborations, including parents assisting children with homework assignments and family members jointly seeking medical information relevant to a loved one. These collaborations can occur at home among immediate family members (e.g., Martha and George), but can also occur remotely when family members are distributed geographically (e.g., Martha and Beth).

Some search tools are designed to support specific user populations, such as Ariadne (Twidale et al., 1997), which is designed to support students working in libraries. It may also be useful for general purpose collaborative search tools to recognize these common populations and adapt to best serve them. This can be done explicitly, with group members stating who they are, but could also be done implicitly. Social or school ties might be identified through social networking services, such as Facebook (http://facebook.com) or Twitter (http://twitter.com), where many friends are often classmates. The presence of connections on a business-oriented social network like LinkedIn (http://www.linkedin.com) might allow the collaborative search tool to automatically infer a professional relationship among the group of searchers and, in turn, impact the type of user interface options shown to or roles assigned to those users.

2.2 RELATIONSHIPS AMONG COLLABORATORS

The relationship among group members is also important to understand when building support for collaborative search. In this section, we look at the direction, strength, and longevity of the relationships commonly present, and we discuss the potential impact of group size.

The relationships among collaborators may be either symmetric or asymmetric, depending on the degree to which the group members share an information need and depending on the role each takes on to address that need. A *symmetric collaboration* is one in which the collaborators share an information need and fulfill the same roles in the search. An *asymmetric collaboration* is one in which the collaborators fulfill different roles. This may arise as a result of a division of a search task into roles based on familiarity with technology, job hierarchy, or specific expertise (Morris and Horvitz, 2007b; Morris et al., 2008; Pickens et al., 2008). It also can arise as a result of asymmetric information needs, where one collaborator enlists the assistance of others. Examples of this include receiving assistance from a reference librarian (Taylor, R., 1968), participating in a guided search experience (e.g., ChaCha (http://www.chacha.com)), and querying a social network (Evans et al., 2010; Morris et al., 2010c).

George and Martha, when searching for common household asthma irritants, run into friction because of the implicit asymmetry of their roles in the search task, with George controlling the computer and Martha looking over his shoulder. Martha gets frustrated that she cannot control what is happening and leaves the collaboration. When they later explicitly partition the task of finding a contractor to inspect their house for mold, they manage instead to use asymmetric roles to their advantage. The roles George and Martha took on when sharing a single computer are often referred to as the "driver" (the user controlling the input devices) and the "observer(s)" (the user(s) looking over the driver's shoulder and making suggestions) (Amershi and Morris, 2008).

A few collaborative search tools are designed specifically to support asymmetric search roles. For example, Cerchiamo (Figure 2.1) supports pairs of users searching together for online video clips. These two users each take on a distinct role – one user acts as the "prospector," discovering new avenues of exploration, while the other acts as the "miner," determining which of these avenues are valuable and exploring them in-depth. These two roles each have distinct user interfaces (Figure 2.2), with the prospector having a rich query-formulation interface and the miner having an interface for rapid serial visual presentation of individual search results.

Another example of system support for asymmetric search roles is Morris et al.'s Smart Splitting system (Morris et al., 2008) (Figure 2.3).

Smart Splitting divides users into roles based on their areas of expertise. Expertise is determined based on the use of personalization techniques (e.g., (Teevan et al., 2005)) which analyze the vocabulary terms present in files on the user's personal computer, as well as the user's past Web history. During a collaborative search, Smart Splitting divides search results such that each collaborator receives the search results most pertinent to his or her expertise. For example, if Martha and her doctor had conducted a joint search to learn more about asthma treatments, Smart Splitting would

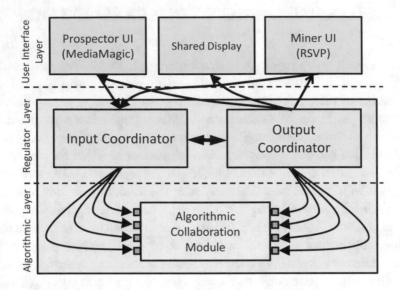

Figure 2.1: Cerchiamo (Pickens et al., 2008) supports asymmetric role-based search for two partners, with one playing the role of the "prospector" and one of the "miner."

Figure 2.2: Cerchiamo (Pickens et al., 2008) supports co-located partners searching online video collections. Each partner has a personal computer displaying role-specific information, and a shared display shows information relevant to both parties.

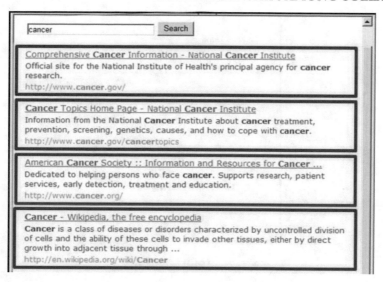

Figure 2.3: The Smart Splitting technique (Morris et al., 2008) adapts personalized search algorithms to divide a search result set among a group of synchronous searchers according to the similarity of the vocabulary in each result to the vocabulary in documents stored on each group member's computer. In this example where two users perform a search on a health topic, one with a technical medical background and one with a lay background, the results highlighted in red would be sent to the searcher with more medical knowledge, whereas the articles written for a lay audience (highlighted in purple) would be sent to her partner.

have sent results containing specialized medical terminology to her doctor's computer, while sending articles written for a more general audience to Martha.

The strength of group members' relationships can impact the success of their collaboration, or the level to which they will engage in equal versus unequal roles in such an effort. Morris et al. (2010c) found that people were more likely to answer information requests from members of their social network whom they felt they had very close relationships with. Techniques such as the one proposed by Gilbert and Karahalios (2009) might be used to predict the strength of collaborators' offline social relationship based on data from social networking tools.

The longevity of a group can also impact the group members' ability to work together. Longevity refers to whether the relationships among group members are short-term (such as based on interest in a specific, shared task) or more permanent (such as based on similarities in personal traits, including sharing a particular hobby or demographic traits). Teevan et al. (2009a) considered how group profiles might be used rank search results so as to identify the most relevant results to the group. They found short term groups formed around the information seeking task to particularly benefit from group-profile-based result ranking techniques. The different group relationships

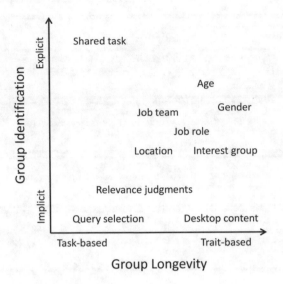

Figure 2.4: The different types of collaborative groups studied by Teevan et al. (2009b), broken down by group longevity and how the group was identified.

Teevan et al. explored can be seen in Figure 2.4. Also shown in the figure is whether the group was identified explicitly, with group members declaring their membership, or implicitly, such as by identifying users with potentially similar interests based on similarity in the queries they issue or results they click on, or based on other factors such as shared employment (e.g., Smyth, B. (2007)). Collaborative search falls on the explicit end of the spectrum.

Group size is another key aspect of group composition that can affect the types of relationships among collaborators, as groups may range from small and intimate to large and potentially unwieldy. Morris, M.R. (2008) found that, for shared-task groups, 80.7% collaborated in pairs while 19.3% worked in groups of three or four members, with none reporting larger group sizes; this lack of larger groups might be an artifact of the lack of tools for supporting such interactions, however. Of course, social search systems that rely on implicit collaboration by users with shared topical interests in order to re-rank results can be used by groups several orders of magnitude larger (e.g., Freyne and Smyth (2006); Teevan et al. (2009b); Smyth et al. (2009)) and, in fact, are typically more useful with larger groups to draw data from.

2.3   WHO: CONCLUSIONS AND FUTURE DIRECTIONS

Understanding the categories of users who most often search collaboratively, and the group configurations used to do so, provides a solid foundation for designing tools to support such users' needs. Knowing that students, families, library patrons, and information workers frequently collaborate on search tasks provides an initial picture of this user landscape, although there is more to be learned. For example, Amershi and Morris (2008, 2009) have found evidence that populations such as the elderly, recent immigrants, and people in developing countries may engage in collaborative search activities, but very little detailed data is currently available on the search needs and practices of these groups. Specific sub-populations of information workers, such as legal professionals (Hansen and Jarvelin, 2005), may also have specialized needs for search tools, and they merit further study. More survey and interview studies to learn about users would be extremely valuable, as much of the current data is drawn from the student and information-worker populations, whose demographics and needs may differ from those of other groups. Gathering data on collaborative tendencies for more detailed demographic factors, such as by gender, age, geography, occupation, education level, or technical expertise, may also facilitate new insights.

In terms of group configuration, few systems take advantage of nuanced relationships among group members, either assuming either peer-based relationships or simple "guided search" relationships. Systems like Cerchiamo (Pickens et al., 2008) with its "prospector" and "miner" roles, or like Smart Splitting (Morris et al., 2008), which considers the expertise areas of each group member, are beginning to uncover the potential for role-tailored group search systems, but this is still a rich and valuable area for further investigation. Reflecting on roles within a collaborative search is an exciting opportunity to design and study systems that support a variety of relationships among group members, such as parents working with children or teachers with their students, as well as in potentially inventing new roles for dividing labor among group members that do not currently exist.

Additionally, although some work has been done on understanding current trends regarding group size, there is room for deeper understanding of not only what size groups users form, but also what size groups are optimal for different tasks, and how group size is being influenced or constrained by current technologies. Understanding how the performance of proposed collaborative search systems scales as group size changes is another open issue.

CHAPTER 3

What?

In this chapter, we explore the motivations behind group searches. We first look at what the common shared search tasks that motivate collaboration are. We then explore what specific aspects of a shared search task lend themselves to collaboration.

3.1   COLLABORATIVE SEARCH TASKS

Researchers have tried to identify common collaborative search tasks via surveys and via the analysis and classification of the tasks collaborative search tools are used for. Table 3.1 shows the common tasks identified by Morris, M.R. (2008) in a survey she conducted of information workers' collaborative search habits, and Table 3.2 shows the common self-generated tasks among groups using the WeSearch system (Morris et al., 2010b).

Table 3.1: 109 information workers who reported cooperating on search using status quo tools described the tasks they had collaborated on, which were then classified into categories of related tasks (Morris et al., 2008).

Task	% of Respondents
Travel planning	27.5%
General shopping tasks	25.7%
Literature search	20.2%
Technical information	16.5%
Fact finding	16.5%
Social planning	12.8%
Medical information	6.4%
Real estate	6.4%

Travel planning was the most common task identified by both, followed by shopping (particularly common among spouses shopping for expensive items such as cars, furniture, real estate, or electronics). Fact-finding (such as in support of a conversation or debate), social planning (e.g., planning large events like weddings and parties, or planning more informal events such as choosing a location for dinner or selecting a movie to view), and finding medical information (e.g., Martha's searches with her family members about her asthma) were also common. Occupation-specific tasks,

Table 3.2: Self-generated collaborative search tasks conducted by 10 groups of co-workers, students, and family members using the WeSearch system (Morris et al., 2010b).

Group Relationship	Task
Colleagues (administrative assistants)	Select the location for their company's next off site meeting.
Colleagues (paralegals)	Conduct background research on a plaintiff in a pending court case.
Colleagues (bankers)	Learn about local businesses who might be in need of financial services.
Colleagues (food scientists)	Research and describe antimicrobial peptides for identifying bacteria.
Colleagues (tech support technicians)	Compile a list of commonly reported problems with a piece of technology commonly utilized by their customers.
Family	Shop for a new home computer.
Family	Plan an upcoming ski trip to Colorado.
Family	Plan an upcoming trip to Montana.
Students	Research treatments for Alzheimer's disease.
Students	Learn about art classes they might take together.

such as retrieving technical information or conducting literature searches were also prevalent among the survey population.

Working on school assignments is another common motivating collaborative search task, as many teachers assign reports to groups to work on together due to pedagogies that emphasize the value of teamwork (Large et al., 2002; Twidale et al., 1997; Amershi and Morris, 2008; Morris et al., 2010b). In addition to students collaborating amongst themselves, Morris, M.R. (2008) found that sometimes parents and children will collaboratively search online together in order for the parent to assist the child with a school homework assignment.

In addition to understanding the tasks that motivate symmetric collaborations on search, some researchers have investigated the goals driving asymmetric collaborations, such as posing a question to one's social network using tools like Facebook and Twitter. For example, Martha might have been able to identify a good company to inspect her house for mold by asking her social network at large, posting the question, "Does anyone know a good mold-removal company?" as her Facebook status. Tables 3.3 and 3.4 show the common question types and topics identified by Morris et al. (2010c) as being asked of one's social network. These were found by surveying 624 social network users for examples of questions they had asked or answered. Subjective information needs, such as seeking recommendations and opinions (51% of questions), were the primary type of question motivating this type of collaborative behavior, although seeking factual knowledge was prevalent as

Table 3.3:   A recent survey of Facebook and Twitter users (Morris et al., 2010c) provided examples of the types of information needs that motivate seeking social assistance with information seeking, by posting the question to a social networking tool. This table shows the percent of 249 example questions that fell into different information need categories, and it provides some examples from the survey data.

Question Type	Percent	Example
Recommendation	29%	Building a new playlist – any ideas for good running songs?
Opinion	22%	I am wondering if I should buy the Kitchen-Aid ice cream maker?
Factual knowledge	17%	Anyone know a way to put Excel charts into LaTeX?
Rhetorical	14%	Is there anything in life you're afraid you won't achieve?
Invitation	9%	Who wants to go to Navya Lounge this evening?
Favor	4%	Needing a babysitter in a big way tonight…anyone??
Social connection	3%	I am hiring in my team. Do you know anyone who would be interested?
Offer	1%	Could any of my friends use boys size 4 jeans?

Table 3.4:   Morris et al. (2010c) survey of Facebook and Twitter users provided data on the topics that people most frequently asked questions about on such services; these topics might represent domains where collaborative search tools could be of assistance. Percentages are out of 249 questions.

Question Topic	Percent	Example
Technology	29%	Anyone know if WoW works on Windows 7?
Entertainment	17%	Was seeing *Up* in the theater worth the money?
Home & Family	12%	So what's the going rate for the tooth fairy?
Professional	11%	Which university is better for Masters? Cornell or Georgia Tech?
Places	8%	Planning a trip to Whistler in the off-season. Recommendation on sites to see?
Restaurants	6%	Hanging in Ballard tonight. Dinner recs?
Current Events	5%	What is your opinion on the recent proposition that was passed in California?
Shopping	5%	What's a good Mother's Day gift?
Ethics & Philosophy	2%	What would you do if you had a week to live?

well (17% of questions). Although the respondents in Morris et al.'s survey were not actively engaged in collaborative searches, their findings suggest that the question topics and types users attempt to address through social means, such as asking one's social network or posting to a Q&A site, might be ones that are in need of more explicit collaborative search support.

The topics of collaborative search tasks differ somewhat from the topics people typically use search engines for. A 2004 study of America Online's query logs (Beitzel et al., 2004) found that the most popular query topics were shopping (13%), entertainment (13%), pornography (10%), computing (9%), health (5%), travel (5%), games (5%), and home (5%). Many popular search engine topics, such as pornography and health, are highly personal. A study of the questions people pose to their social networks (Morris et al., 2010c) suggests that those topics, along with religion, politics, dating, and financial issues, were ones on which people may be particularly careful about whom they collaborate with.

Via query log analysis, Broder, A. (2002) identified three kinds of common intents people have while searching: informational (intended to find a piece of information), transactional (intended to perform some action), and navigational (intended to find a particular resource). Collaborative search intents can be viewed within this taxonomy as well. For example, while students tend to collaborate mostly on informational searches, seniors and new immigrants also collaborated with other, more technically skilled searchers, on transactional (e.g., paying bills) and navigational tasks (e.g., finding sites with job postings) (Amershi and Morris, 2008).

3.2   COLLABORATIVE STRATEGIES AND TACTICS

Although Web search is typically thought of in terms of entering a keyword into a search engine, Web search behavior is usually much more complex, encompassing a larger process of formulating and refining an information need, selecting appropriate resources, and evaluating and using the information one has found. Social interactions can play important roles at each of many stages of an information seeking task.

When searching, people employ a number of different search *strategies*. A search strategy is plan for how the searcher will go about finding the information that is being sought. For example, Martha's initial strategy to learn more about asthma after her diagnosis was to browse quickly through many diverse online asthma-related resources to get a big-picture understanding of the disease. Search strategies can vary greatly, ranging from orienteering to the information target using clues from the information environment, to teleporting directly to the target by fully describing it up front (Teevan et al., 2004).

Bates, M. (1979a,b) introduced the notion of search *tactics*, or specific actions that assist a user in implementing a search strategy. Entering a query into a search engine, for example, is usually just one tactic in a larger search strategy (Teevan et al., 2004). Bates, M. (1979a,b) defined 29 search tactics, including ones that involve thinking about how to implement a search strategy (e.g., *weigh*: make a cost-benefit assessment of potential actions), formulating an information need (e.g., *reduce*: subtract terms from a query), and using the information resources found (e.g., *stretch*: use an information resource for a purpose other than its intended one). While Bates' tactics focus on the single-searcher scenario, some of them nonetheless recognize the role of the social in information seeking. For example, the *consult* tactic involves asking a colleague for suggestions. The *brainstorm* tactic involves generating many ideas, which, while not explicitly collaborative, certainly often is. And the *bibble* tactic involves looking for ready-prepared bibliographies, or, in other words, reusing material already found by trusted others. Bates' inclusion of tactics such as these reveals the importance of social interactions in everyday information seeking processes.

Twidale et al. (1997) observed the way students used computer terminals to find information in a university library, noting several types of collaborative interactions. Based on these observations, they recommended aspects of information seeking where social interactions could play a role, with an eye toward reminding the designers of emerging digital library systems of the importance of preserving the types of social interactions that were possible in traditional library settings. Twidale et al. distinguished two collaborative search strategies: *process-related* collaboration (collaboration on how to find information) and *product-related* collaboration (where the collaboration involves exchanging the sought-after information itself). They also reported several specific tactics people used to implement these strategies, which are described in Table 3.5.

Researchers have built on these explorations of traditional collaborative library practices by exploring the tactics people use to search for digital information collaboratively. Morris, M.R. (2008) surveyed 204 information workers about when they used Web search tools, including search engines and hyperlinks, to search collaboratively. She identified several specific search tactics where users engaged in social activities. These included observing another's Web search over-the-shoulder and suggesting alternate query terms, instant-messaging with other users to coordinate real-time information seeking in remote scenarios, and explicitly dividing up responsibilities for a search task among several people and then sharing the results of one's assigned sub-task with the group. Like Bates and Twidale et al., Morris also found that brainstorming with others, particularly brainstorming alternative query keyword choices, was a common social interaction during information seeking tasks.

Morris' survey also identified common tactics in which users interacted with others to share the products of an information seeking task, summarized in Table 3.6. These included sending a list of links or textual summary of findings over email or printing them to share with someone in person, using the telephone to share search findings verbally, turning one's computer monitor or connecting a computer to a projector to share screen contents with a co-located user, and creating a webpage, Wiki, or other electronic document to record one's search findings in a format re-usable by others.

Evans and Chi (2008) surveyed 150 people using Mechanical Turk, asking these users to answer questions about their most recent information seeking experience. Based on these findings, they proposed breaking down the opportunities for social interaction during information seeking into three categories: *before search*, *during search*, and *after search* (in contrast with the two-category *process/product* dichotomy used by Twidale et al. and Morris). Their model is illustrated in Figure 3.1. Evans and Chi then identified several tactics in which their survey respondents used social resources

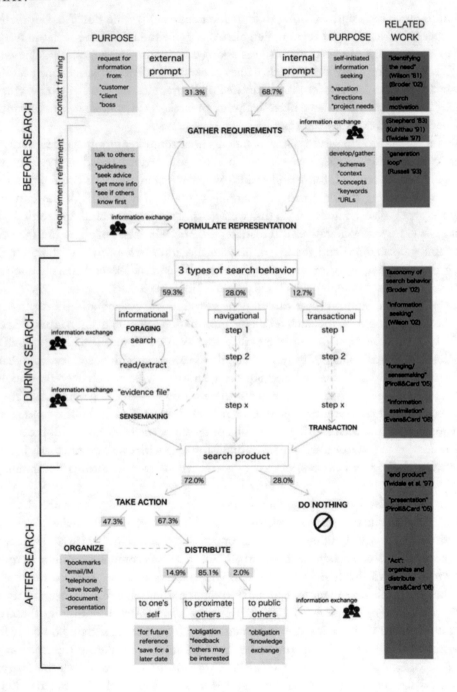

Figure 3.1: Evans and Chi (2008) modeled the stages at which 150 survey participants reported engaging in social interactions before, during, and after a Web search.

Table 3.5: Twidale et al. (1997) identified several tactics used by students in a university library for collaborating on specific aspects of the process and products of searching.

Tactic	Search Stage	Description
Do You Know?	Process	asking a known individual for a specific piece of information or for assistance with a specific aspect of the search process
Does Anyone Know?	Process	broadcasting a request for help to a large audience rather than to a specific individual, such as via an email list
Who Might Know?	Process	attempting to identify a specific expert who might have the desired process or product knowledge
Remote Help	Process	interaction with a specific, though personally unknown, individual whose job is to provide information seeking assistance, such as a remote reference librarian
Joint Searching	Process	sharing a computer terminal with another user or users, working together on the same task
Coordinated Searching	Process	working with another user (each with his own computer terminal) on related tasks, and exchanging information as needed
Brainstorming	Process	working with others to generate new approaches when current information seeking strategies are unsuccessful
Making Contacts	Process	meeting other library users with shared interests who might assist a user with future information needs, such as noticing that someone else has checked out the same book as they did
Personal Recommendation	Products	sharing a found item with known individuals who might find it interesting
Annotation	Products	augmenting found information with personal insights or comments that might later be useful to others
Releasing an Information Package	Products	assembling the results of a complex search into a form that could be reused by others (which could then enable a later user to utilize Bates' "bibble" tactic)

at each of these stages, described in Table 3.7.

By studying users in traditional libraries and users of single-user Web search tools, Bates, Twidale et al., Morris, and Evans and Chi were able to identify what specific aspects of an information seeking task invite collaboration. Although some of the specifics of their classifications

Table 3.6: The percentage of 204 information workers completing a survey on Web search habits who had engaged in several specific collaborative actions (Morris et al., 2008).

Collaborative Activity	Respondents
Collaboration on Search *Process*	90.2%
Watched over someone's shoulder as he/she searched the Web, and suggested alternate query terms.	87.7%
Instant-messaged other people to coordinate real-time Web information-seeking.	30.4%
Divided up responsibilities for a search task among several people, and then shared the results.	18.1%
Collaboration on Search *Products*	96.1%
E-mailed someone links to share the results of a Web search.	86.3%
Showed a personal display to other people to share the results of a Web search.	85.3%
E-mailed someone a textual summary to share the results of a Web search.	60.3%
Called someone on the phone to tell them about the results of a Web search.	49.0%
Printed webpages on paper to share the results of a Web search.	41.2%
Created a document (other than a webpage or email) to share the results of a Web search.	34.3%
Used a large form-factor or projected display to share the results of a Web search.	24.5%
Created or posted to a webpage to share the results of a Web search.	15.2%

differ, there are many commonalities, including the realization that collaboration occurs both over the process of search (preparing for and executing the search) and over the products of search (understanding and disseminating the results found). Researchers developing systems to better support collaboration on search sometimes focus on designing systems to support integrating social interactions throughout all stages of a search task (e.g., SearchTogether (Morris and Horvitz, 2007b)), and sometimes focus on supporting one of these more specific opportunities for collaboration (e.g., CoSense (Paul and Morris, 2009), see Figure 3.2). Both are potentially valuable approaches to enhancing the experience of digital information seeking.

It is worth noting, however, that just as not all aspects of an individual's search happen individually, not all actions related to satisfying a collaborative information task take place collaboratively (Bruce et al., 2002). For example, as observed by Morris, M.R. (2008), collaborators sometimes employ a divide and conquer strategy, breaking down the task into pieces each collaborator can fulfill alone, without collaboration. Martha and George do this when they partition the task of finding

Table 3.7: Evans and Chi (2008) identified tactics information workers used to collaborate with others before, during, and after search.

Tactic	Search Stage	Description
Context Framing	Before Search	This opportunity for social interaction refers to the context motivating the information seeking task, which may be self-generated but also may be externally generated, such as due to a request from a manager, client, or friend.
Requirement Refinement	Before Search	This stage involves understanding the task in detail, which may involve iterating on the task description with others (such as if the search was due to an external request).
Foraging	During Search	When foraging, searchers assimilate information they have found and use it to iterate on their search, such as by using new keywords they discover in initial results; opportunities for social interaction include brainstorming keyword refinements with others.
Sensemaking	During Search	Sensemaking involves evaluating information as it is found and assessing whether the search goal has been achieved (Russell et al., 1993). Some researchers have explored more specifically the role that collaboration might play in sensemaking during the search process, developing specialized tools such as CoSense (Paul and Morris, 2009) to support such interactions (see Figure 3.2).
Organizing and Distributing Information	After Search	This tactic involves organizing found information, such as by collecting a list of links or creating a summary document or webpage. This often was a step toward sharing this organized content with others, either face-to-face, by telephone, or through electronic means of distribution.

a good contractor to remove the mold from their house. Generally, search strategies that involve sharing the product of a search rather than the process involve many individual actions. Thus, many collaborative search tools are designed to support a collaborator's individual actions as well as the more group-oriented aspects of collaborative search.

3.3   WHAT: CONCLUSIONS AND FUTURE DIRECTIONS

Understanding users' motivating tasks and the specific aspects of these tasks that provide collaboration opportunities is key to developing appropriate collaborative search tools. Much of our knowledge of popular collaborative tasks comes from the information-worker population (e.g., (Morris, M.R.,

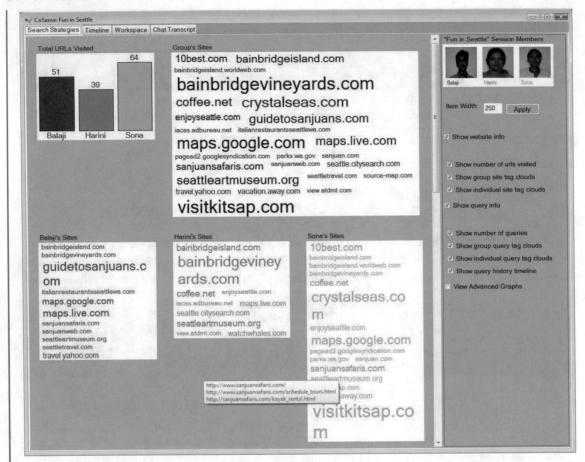

Figure 3.2: CoSense (Paul and Morris, 2009) is a tool designed specifically to support the sensemaking stage of remote collaborative search, by offering rich visualizations of both the search process and products.

2008; Evans and Chi, 2008)); studying the tasks of more diverse user groups may shed light on additional high-value collaboration scenarios, as well as further our understanding of what tasks are common across multiple populations. The study of and reflection on the underlying structure of tasks (e.g., (Bates, M., 1979a,b; Evans and Chi, 2008)) is another valuable avenue for further investigation, as understanding what aspects of tasks involve interactions with others may be indicative of which features will be most highly valued in collaborative search systems.

CHAPTER 4

Where?

In addition to knowing who is searching and what aspects of their task might benefit from collaboration, another important dimension of collaborative search to consider is where the participants are located relative to other collaborators. Group members may be *remote* (in distinct locations) or *co-located* (physically co-present). Although most collaborative search systems are designed around exclusively remote or co-located scenarios, *mixed-presence* arrangements, in which a subset of the group is co-located while others are remote, are also possible. In this chapter, we explore the issues that different participant configurations raise for collaborative search systems, and discuss example systems designed to support these different group arrangements.

4.1 REMOTE COLLABORATION

Often, users with shared information needs are in separate locations. For example, Martha and her sister Beth worked together to learn more about Martha's asthma even though they were in separate locations, and Martha and her husband George attempted to remotely identify a company to inspect their house for mold while both were at their respective workplaces. Currently, co-searchers either send lists of links back and forth over email, like Beth and Martha did, or use the phone or instant messaging in order to attempt to coordinate their actions, like Martha and George did (Morris, M.R., 2008). However, such arrangements are challenging due to limited awareness of and context about other group members' activities. Several solutions have been proposed to enhance the experience of remote collaboration on Web search. In this section, after providing brief overviews of these systems, we discuss one example, SearchTogether, in more depth.

Collaborative Web browsers (Cabri et al., 1999; Gianoutsos and Grundy, 1996; Greenberg and Roseman, 1996) are one type of system that can be used to support remote co-searching, although they are designed for collaborative browsing and lack search-specific features. Typically, collaborative browsers support synchronous collaboration via yoked views, where one user's navigation causes other group members' browsers to automatically follow suit. Often, there is a master/slave relationship among co-browsers, where only one group member's browser causes other users to follow. For example, Cabri et al.'s group browsing system (Cabri et al., 1999) consisted of a two-frame browser, with one frame showing the group's jointly-viewed webpage and the other showing a history of the group's page visits, as well as chat. The W4 browser (Gianoutsos and Grundy, 1996) provided follow-me navigation and scrolling, remote telepointers, and chat. GroupWeb (Greenberg and Roseman, 1996) is another co-browsing system that enabled yoked browsing and telepointers; collaborators could also associate comments with jointly-viewed pages.

A variety of social media can also be used to support remote collaboration on a search task. Social media enables users to share links or thoughts about online content with others; like co-browsers, these systems are not specifically targeted at supporting Web search, but can be used to support some related functionality such as link-sharing or commenting. For example, the Sociable Web (Donath and Robertson, 1994) and Community Bar (http://www.communitybar.net) are systems that allow a user to know when others are currently viewing the same webpage; they can then initiate a chat with those users about that page's content. Systems for sharing bookmarks include WebTagger (Keller et al., 1997), Wittenburg et al.'s system (Wittenburg et al., 1995), and commercial sites such as del.icio.us (http://del.icio.us).

Users can also participate in remotely-guided search experiences, such as receiving help from a reference librarian (Taylor, R., 1968); online services such as QuestionPoint (http://www.oclc.org/questionpoint) enable this experience even when the librarian is remote. Some search engines, such as Cha Cha (http://www.chacha.com) route users' queries to human beings who help them find answers, although such systems are often designed as cost-effective ways to simulate natural language processing rather than as true collaborative tools.

There are also systems designed specifically to support remote collaboration on search tasks. Such systems generally provide some support both for working together on the process of searching (e.g., selecting query terms, selecting search sources) as well as for collaborating on the products of searching (e.g., identifying content that is most relevant).

Some collaborative search tools are designed for special-purpose databases. For example, C-TORI (Hoppe and Zhao, 1994) allows a group to collaborate when searching over a relational database, and MUSE [Krishnappa, 2005] and MUSE (Krishnappa, R., 2005) allows pairs of users to search over a medical database.

Systems have also begun to emerge to support more general purpose collaborative search over the Web. SearchTogether (Morris and Horvitz, 2007b), discussed in more detail below, is one such system. HeyStaks (Smyth et al., 2009) (Figure 4.1) is another example; HeyStaks allows users to share "staks" of relevant content with collaborators with similar interests, and the results they click impact the ranking of results when their collaborators execute similar queries. S^3 (Morris and Horvitz, 2007a) allows users to asynchronously collaborate on search tasks by treating a search session (including keywords, results, and comments on found pages) as a file that can be saved and loaded using the special S^3 browser; these files can be emailed among collaborators in a manner analogous to other types of office documents. CIRE (Romano et al., 1999) (Figure 4.2) allows users to search singly, but enables them to attach comments to the pages they have found, which are then visible to other group members who encounter those pages later.

Implicit information about collaborators' searches, including clicks, queries, and other actions, can also be shared to group members to provide increased awareness of other's activities. For example, with *group hit highlighting* (Morris et al., 2008), not only are an individual's query terms highlighted

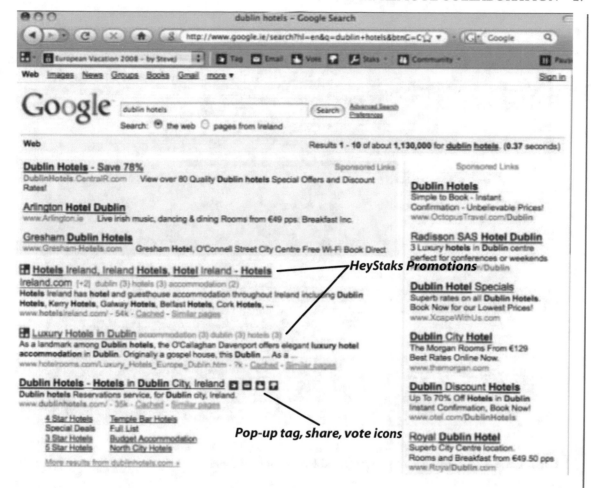

Figure 4.1: HeyStaks (Smyth et al., 2009) is a browser plug-in that allows remote collaboration among groups of users, who can share "starks" of content with people having similar interests.

in the search results for a query, but so are the query terms of collaborators. An example can be seen in Figure 4.3. Group hit highlighting can serve to help draw the searcher's attention to relevant results that might not have otherwise been obvious. For instance, in our introductory scenario, when Beth was searching for information about her sister's asthma, if she had been using a system with group hit highlighting she might have been made aware of her sister's interest in mold and other household irritants when terms like "mold" ended up highlighted in her general search results for "asthma triggers." Exposure of links Martha had clicked on would further help Beth avoid duplicating effort her sister had already expended.

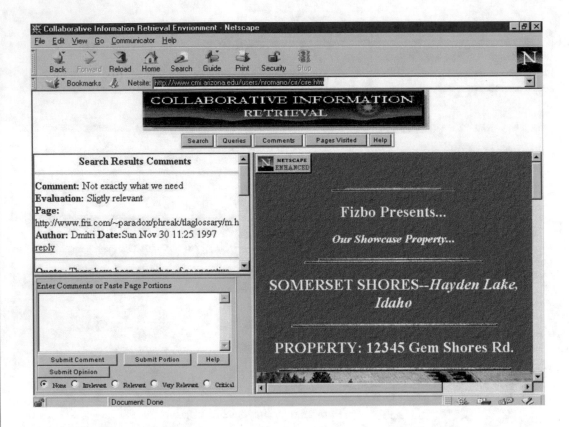

Figure 4.2: CIRE (Romano et al., 1999) enabled remote collaborators to share comments on webpages.

Asthma Triggers
Asthma Triggers – <u>Molds</u>, U. S. Environmental Protection Agency; **Asthma Triggers** -
<u>Dust</u> Mites, U. S. Environmental Protection Agency; Asthma Triggers - Secondhand
Smoke, U ...
healthandenergy.com/asthma_triggers.htm

Figure 4.3: Group hit-highlighting (Morris et al., 2008) can be used to draw users' attention to search results that match both their own and their collaborators' queries. In this example, terms from a participant's query are shown in bold, and terms from collaborators' queries are underlined.

4.1.1   EXAMPLE: SEARCHTOGETHER

SearchTogether enables remote collaboration among small groups of users, working either synchronously or asynchronously on Web search tasks. A screenshot of the system is shown in Figure 4.4. SearchTogether was designed to support remote collaboration by including features to support *awareness*, *division of labor*, and *persistence*.

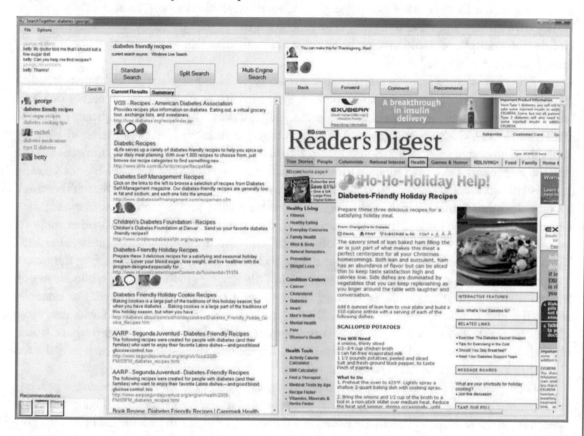

Figure 4.4: SearchTogether (Morris and Horvitz, 2007b) supports remote collaboration (both synchronous and asynchronous) among groups of users. The left column of the interface contains integrated chat, a group query history, and the recommendations queue. The central column enables standard or automatic-division-of-labor searching, and provides metadata-augmented views of search results. The right column displays the current webpage, augmented with other group members' metadata, and provides facilities for attaching comments and ratings to pages.

As discussed earlier regarding group hit highlighting, awareness of other group members' activities can help make collaborative search a more lightweight interaction by reducing the need for explicitly asking other group members for routine information, such as their recent queries. Such awareness can also reduce undesired redundancy of effort, such as when multiple group members use the same keywords unintentionally. SearchTogether's Query Awareness region, shown in Figure 4.5, provides per-user query histories in order to help users maintain awareness of others' search strategies. Page-specific metadata, shown in Figure 4.6, is also provided to support awareness among remote collaborators. This works by augmenting search results pages and other webpages with icons indicating which (if any) other group members have already visited a page, as well as any positive or negative ratings and comments they may have given the page. This information can help users decide, for example, to avoid visiting results that they can see other group members have already tried and found to not be helpful.

Division of labor features help group members to avoid unnecessary redundant work and to parallelize work among group members, perhaps suited to each user's specific skill set. For example, more tech-savvy searchers may be skilled at formulating queries while their less technically proficient collaborators can work on triaging results. SearchTogether facilitates flexible division of labor by including integrated instant messaging features, to allow users to converse about strategies as they search; such chats are stored along with the search session so that they are available for viewing by asynchronous collaborators, as well. Another way to divide labor is through SearchTogether's recommendation feature, which enables a user to push a particular webpage to another user; such recommendations are queued up in a special area of the interface. Finally, SearchTogether supports automatic division of labor through its "split search" and "multi-engine search" features. For each of these features, one group member types a query, and the results are divided among the group. For split search, the results are divided round-robin style among group members while for multi-engine search each group member receives results from a different search source. For example, if Martha and her sister used SearchTogether to research asthma treatments, Martha may have chosen to divide the search results such that she received results from a general-purpose search engine, while her sister received results from a health-focused vertical provider, such as PubMed (http://www.ncbi.nlm.nih.gov/pubmed).

The persistence features in SearchTogether are designed to facilitate asynchronous collaboration, a phenomenon which is discussed in greater detail in the next chapter. All content from a SearchTogether session is persistently stored in a database so that it can be accessed by remote collaborators. Additionally, SearchTogether can automatically generate a search summary. An example summary is shown in Figure 4.7. This artifact is meant to create an archival representation of the search's key findings, which can be shared with a broader circle of collaborators. For example, the default summary includes all pages that any group members gave a positive rating or comment to. For each page in the summary, the title, thumbnail, and list of visiting group members is displayed, as well as their comments and ratings. The summary provides links back to each of the original pages mentioned.

Evaluations of SearchTogether found that awareness features were particularly important to remote collaborators, as was the ability to export summaries of a group's sessions. Automatic division of labor was less frequently used, although it remains to be seen whether smarter division

Figure 4.5: SearchTogethers' group query history helps facilitate lightweight awareness of other group members' search strategies. This awareness may be helpful for reducing undesired redundant efforts, as well as for helping users reformulate their queries by exposing them to others' syntax and synonyms. The query histories are interactive, and can be used as shortcuts to view the results found by other group members.

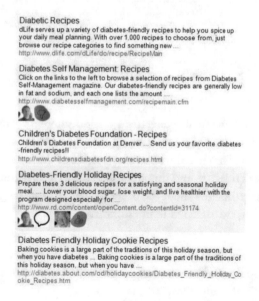

Figure 4.6: SearchTogether augments search results with several types of metadata. Visitation awareness information provides an image of a group member adjacent to any search results they have visited. If a group member has provided a rating ("thumbs down" for negative or "thumbs up" for positive) or added a comment to a page, these are also indicated via icons. This metadata can help users triage search results; for example, they may wish to avoid re-visiting sites already visited by other group members, or they may wish to specifically visit such sites when a group member indicates there is information of value there.

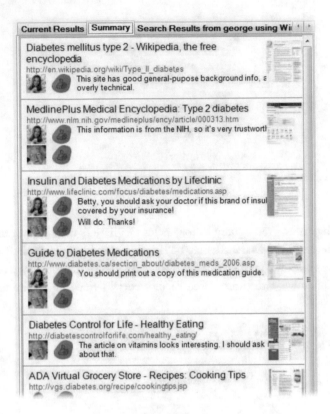

Figure 4.7: SearchTogether automatically generates a session summary. This interactive summary provides quick access to the most relevant content found by group members, as well as providing an overview of the search that can be exported or shared with others outside of the immediate group of collaborators. The summary includes a page's title, url, and thumbnail, as well as information about which group members have visited and what they thought about the page. By default, only pages that have received at least one comment or positive rating are included in the summary.

algorithms (e.g., "smart splitting," which can split results based on similarity to content on each user's computer (Morris et al., 2008)), and greater familiarity with the collaborative search paradigm will change the perceived benefit of such features.

4.2   CO-LOCATED COLLABORATION

There are many situations in which users with shared information needs are co-located. Such situations may be planned (e.g., students working together in the library or co-workers meeting in a conference room) or spontaneous (e.g., friends gathering in a café or family members relaxing in their living room). Amershi and Morris (2009) conducted diary studies describing incidents of co-located collaborative searches both in office and home settings; they found that while some co-located searches were quite involved, lasting many minutes or hours, a majority were rather brief, serendipitous events, lasting only a few minutes. Based on the findings of their study, they recommend that designers of systems for co-located searching keep system start-up costs minimal, provide a history of a group's suggestions, enable distribution of control among group members, include consensus facilities, provide awareness mechanisms and shared context, and make it easy for each participant to take relevant information away from the shared setting.

Researchers have begun to explore how to support co-located search scenarios using the different resources that may be available in different co-located settings (e.g., personal computers, mobile devices, large displays). In this section, we first give an overview of the range of solutions that have been explored for supporting co-located collaborative search. We then explore two such systems, CoSearch and WeSearch, in-depth, in order to illustrate the unique design considerations that must be considered when designing for co-located groups.

Systems for co-located collaborative search tend to include a separate input device for each group member, oftentimes augmented by a shared display. For example, Cerchiamo (Pickens et al., 2008) (Figure 2.2) supports co-located collaboration among a pair of users searching over a video archive. Each partner uses his own PC, which shows the individual information relevant to that user's distinct role in the search task (either entering query terms as the "prospector" or triaging results as the "miner"). Cerchiamo supplements these personal computers with a large, shared wall display that shows data relevant to both users (i.e., the overall progress of the search task). WebGlance (Paek et al., 2004) (Figure 4.8) supports co-located Web browsing, although it doesn't focus on search *per se*. Users can control a Web browser on a large, shared display, by sending commands from their PDAs. Maekawa et al. (2006) (Figure 4.9) support visual search of a webpage by dividing a large page into non-overlapping sections and sending one section to each group member's mobile device, enabling a divide-and-conquer approach. Query By Argument (Blackwell et al., 2004) (Figure 4.10) is an educational system focused on rhetorical argument construction, that provides students with RFID-tagged tangible objects representing key concepts from a document collection; manipulating these tangibles re-ranks the relevance of items in the collection, helping students to see which information might support their current arguments. CoSearch (Amershi and Morris, 2008) combines group members' mobile phones with a shared display to support collaborative Web search; we discuss CoSearch in-depth below.

While some of the aforementioned systems used shared displays, they all provided individual devices (phones, PDAs, PCs, or tangibles) for each group member. However, as touch-sensitive devices have increased in prevalence, researchers have also begun to explore how a single, shared multi-touch display can support collaborative search (generally in a tabletop form-factor, so as to enable face-to-face work). Morris et al. (2010a) described the design space of surface computing systems that support co-located collaborative search (Table 4.1). Their design space considers two primary dimensions: the group's configuration (such as the size of group supported, the spatial arrangement of group members, the ecology of devices they bring with them to the shared display,

Figure 4.8: WebGlance (Paek et al., 2004) enabled co-located users to share control of a Web browser on a public display by using their personal PDAs.

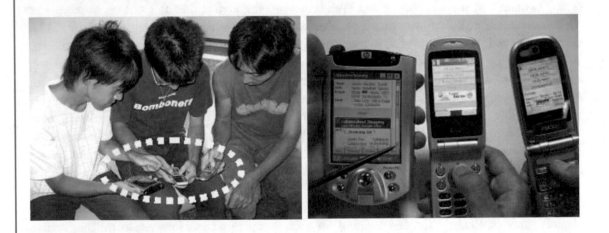

Figure 4.9: A collaborative Web browsing system for mobile phone users (Maekawa et al., 2006) supports dividing up a webpage into several segments so that each user can view a different segment simultaneously on his small-screen device, simplifying visual search when groups of users are out and about without large displays (© 2006 IEEE).

Figure 4.10: The Query By Argument system (Blackwell et al., 2004) provided a tangible interface for co-located information retrieval.

and their working style), and the nature of the search task supported (such as the specific application domain, types of inputs provided to the search system, and stages of the search process supported).

Físchlár-DT (Smeaton et al., 2006), for example, enables group members to search video collections using a touch-sensitive, top-projected tabletop display. As shown in Figure 4.11, users type keywords on the tabletop using virtual keyboards, and they can manipulate matching keyframes using direct-touch interactions. The Personal Digital Historian (Shen et al., 2002), seen in Figure 4.12, is designed to support collaborative photo browsing and storytelling on a single touch-screen. It enables groups to query a tagged photo collection by filtering along the dimensions "who," "what," "where," and "when." TeamSearch (Morris et al., 2006) (Figure 4.13) is another tabletop photo-searching system. TeamSearch enables group members to manipulate virtual tokens in order to create a visual boolean representation of a query. Cambiera (Isenberg and Fisher, 2009) (Figure 4.14) enables pairs of users to search over a document collection on a Microsoft Surface (http://www.microsoft.com/surface), providing compact visualizations of search results in order to save space on the shared display and indicate overlap among pairs' result sets. FourBySix Search (Hartmann et al., 2009; Morris et al., 2010a) (Figure 4.15) enables the use of physical keyboards placed atop a shared tabletop system; the relative distances of the keyboards impacts whether typed query terms are interpreted separately or jointly, and their relative orientations impact whether

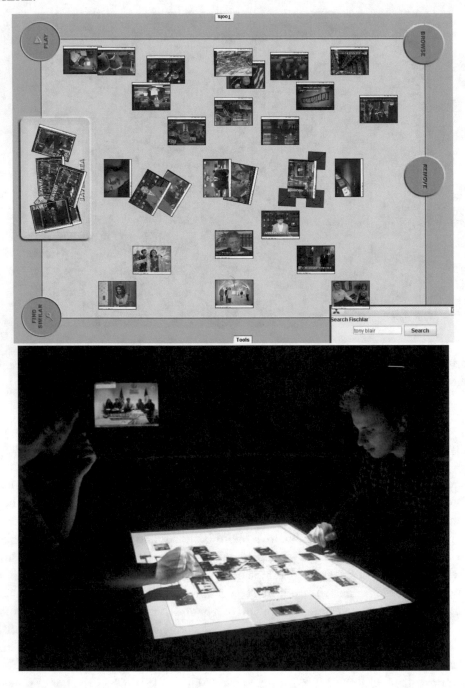

Figure 4.11: Físchlár-DT (Smeaton et al., 2006) supports co-located collaboration on video search using a multitouch tabletop.

Figure 4.12: The Personal Digital Historian (Shen et al., 2002) supports colocated exploration of digital photo collections by enabling group members to filter a collection along the *who, what, where,* and *when* dimensions.

Figure 4.13: TeamSearch (Morris et al., 2006) supports co-located collaborative image search among four-person groups using a touch-sensitive tabletop display by enabling group members to collaboratively construct Boolean queries using virtual *query tokens*.

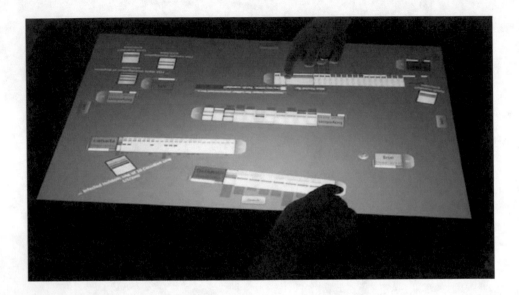

Figure 4.14: Cambiera (Isenberg and Fisher, 2009) uses information visualization techniques, such as collaborative brushing and linking, to compactly represent search results when co-located partners share a tabletop display.

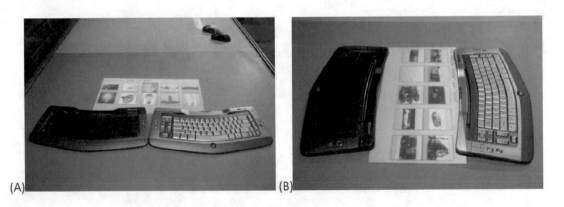

(A)   (B)

Figure 4.15: FourBySix Search (Morris et al., 2010a) uses the relative position and orientation of users' keyboards to define the semantics of their search. (A) A side-by-side configuration broadens the search (disjunctive). (B) A face-to-face configuration narrows the search (conjunctive).

Table 4.1: Design space of collaborative search applications for tabletop displays (Morris et al., 2010a).

Group Configuration					
Collaborative Style	Tightly-coupled	Transitioning	Parallel work		
Group size	Pairs	Small teams	Large groups		
Location	Co-located	Distributed	Mixed-presence		
Device ecology	Table	Table + additional outputs/displays	Table + Additional input devices/objects	Import data	Export data
Search Task					
Application domain	Web	Multimedia	Personal documents	Database	
Search inputs	Keywords	Visual language	Touch/Gestures	Tangible	A.I.
Analysis stages	Search	Sensemaking	Reporting		

joint queries are interpreted conjunctively (keyboards facing each other) or disjunctively (keyboards side-by-side). WebSurface (Tuddenham et al., 2009) (Figure 4.16) supports co-located Web browsing by providing users with a high-resolution projected display; clicking links opens pages in a separate browser window, so that related pages can be viewed side-by-side on the large surface for easy comparison. WeSearch (Morris et al., 2010b) is a tabletop system designed to support not only collaborative Web searching, but also the accompanying group sensemaking task; WeSearch is discussed in greater detail below.

While systems such as WeSearch and WebSurface employ shared displays in order to take advantage of a face-to-face work arrangement, sometimes co-located collaborators employ shared displays not out of preference but due to resource limitations. Although computers have become more plentiful in recent years, shared computer use remains common in many settings. For example, in U.S. public schools, the ratio of students to computers is 3.8 to 1 (U.S. Dept. of Education, 2006a), and the number of Internet-enabled computers available in U.S. public libraries is 3 for every 5,000 people (U.S. Dept. of Education, 2006b). In developing countries, these ratios can be even more skewed. For example, in rural schools in developing countries, the student-to-computer ratio can be as high 10 to 1 (Pawar et al., 2006). Even when resource constraints are not a factor, the social and pedagogical benefits of face-to-face collaboration and shared viewing of information can be a compelling reason for collaborators to share a single computer (Stewart et al., 1999). For example, in a recent survey of 204 Microsoft employees, 87.7% reported engaging in "backseat driver" searches where they watched over another person's shoulder and suggest query terms to try or links to click (Morris, M.R., 2008).

Figure 4.16: WebSurface (Tuddenham et al., 2009) supports co-located collaborative Web browsing using a high-resolution projected tabletop, enabling side-by-side comparison and spatial grouping of related pages.

4.2.1   EXAMPLE: COSEARCH

The CoSearch system (Amershi and Morris, 2008) provides an example of how a system can support co-located collaboration by providing separate input devices to each group member, in order to enable distributed control. CoSearch was designed for the scenario where a group of users gathers around a shared PC to search the Web, as often occurs in classrooms and libraries.

By interviewing several teachers and librarians, the designers of CoSearch identified several limitations to conducting collaborative searches by sharing a single PC, described in Table 4.2.

Several of these difficulties arose for Martha and George when they searched together at home for common household irritants. George initially ignored Martha's suggestion about what link he should click, making it difficult for Martha to contribute. And when they found a page discussing common household molds, the two encountered a pacing problem – George scrolled through the page too fast for Martha to read.

To address these shortcomings of status quo search tools, Amershi and Morris designed CoSearch (Figure 4.17), which supplements the shared PC with input from multiple mice and/or mobile phones in order to distribute control of the search task among all group members. CoSearch's two primary user interfaces are CoSearchPC, shown in Figure 4.18, which runs on the shared

Figure 4.17: CoSearch (Amershi and Morris, 2008) supports co-located collaborative search by providing each group member with a personal input device (either a mouse or mobile phone) with which they can jointly control a shared PC.

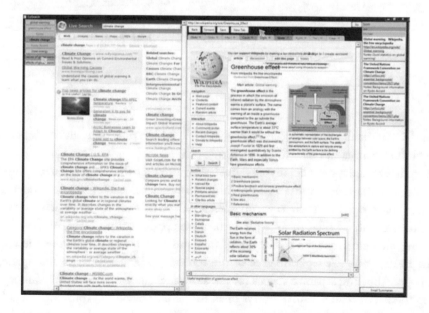

Figure 4.18: CoSearch uses a specially-designed browser on the shared PC that provides each group member with a distinct, colorcoded cursor. Queuing mechanisms for queries and pages enable effective distribution of control.

Table 4.2: Amershi and Morris (2008) interviewed teachers and librarians to identify the limitations students face when searching jointly using a single, shared computer.

Challenge	Description
Difficulties Contributing	Group members without access to the computer's mouse and keyboard must rely on the "driver" to act upon their suggestions. Conversely, "drivers" may be so busy carrying out others' suggestions that they do not have time to propose their own ideas.
Lack of Awareness	More dominant or vocal group members can overshadow others' contributions.
Lack of Hands-On Learning	Group members not controlling the PC's input devices lose an opportunity to gain direct skills with technology.
Pacing Problems	The user operating the input devices may change or scroll webpages too quickly or slowly for other group members' reading abilities.
Referential Difficulties	Pointing at the shared display to establish context or refer to specific on-screen items may be difficult depending on group size and configuration.
Single-Track Strategies	Although different group members might have different search strategies (e.g., different query terms they want to try or different links they think the group should follow), the shared display requires the group to follow only a single path through the information space.
Information Loss	At the end of the collaborative session, group members have no record of what they have accomplished to take with them.

computer, and CoSearchMobile, shown in Figure 4.19, which runs on each user's personal mobile phone. The phones connect to the PC using Bluetooth.

CoSearchPC displays a specially-designed Web browser that uses queueing mechanisms in order to handle simultaneous inputs from each group member. Each group member is associated with a distinct color, and has their own on-screen cursor in that color. When users enter query terms (using the keypad on their mobile phones), these appear, color-coded, in the browser's query queue. Clicking an item from the query queue executes that query, displaying the current search results in the results pane. A separate area of the browser, adjacent to the results pane, shows the current webpage. Allotting separate spaces for the search results and the current webpage is done in order to keep the list of search results always open for perusal by other group members. The current webpage is just one of several tabs in the page queue. Tabs are color-coded to indicate which group member clicked the link to open them (by using their phone's joystick to move their individual cursors). Group members can use the notes region to augment any webpage with notes, which can be downloaded to each group member's phone as a post-meeting take-away.

Figure 4.19: CoSearch users' mobile phones connect to the shared PC over Bluetooth, and can be used to type query terms and send them to the PC, to control a mouse cursor on the PC, to view individual webpages, and to download session notes.

Evaluations of CoSearch found that it addressed the aforementioned limitations of shared-computer searching, while preserving high communication and awareness levels among groups as compared with providing each group member with their own, side-by-side, PC.

Since, as mentioned earlier, computer-sharing for searches often occurs in resource-constrained environments, it is possible that users may not have Web-enabled mobile phones with which to operate a system like CoSearch. For this reason, CoSearch also offers a subset of its functionality by connecting multiple mice to a single computer. This enables multi-cursor operations, such as enqueuing links in the page queue, but eliminates features that require text entry, such as simultaneous query entry capabilities. Understanding how to better support simultaneous search with impoverished input devices is an important area of future work for many resource-constrained settings, such as schools or internet kiosks in the developing world. Work on text-entry techniques for multi-mouse setups (Amershi et al., 2010) is one example of an advance that could be used to enrich future multi-mouse collaborative search tools.

4.2.2   EXAMPLE: WESEARCH

The WeSearch system (Morris et al., 2010b) provides an example of how a collaborative search tool can support co-located collaboration in a system with a single, shared device. WeSearch was designed to support face-to-face collaborative search on tabletop displays, an emerging form factor operated by touch input. Based on a review of the challenges of using tabletop systems for productivity tasks, Morris et al. designed WeSearch in order to mitigate the challenges of cluttering the shared display, reading text at odd orientations, and typing on virtual keyboards. Additionally, WeSearch was designed not only to support the process stages of collaborative Web search but also subsequent collaborative sensemaking.

WeSearch supports up to four group members, gathered around a four-foot-wide by six-foot-long standing-height, top-projected tabletop, shown in Figure 4.20. Each group member has

Figure 4.20: WeSearch (Morris et al., 2010b) supports co-located collaborative search around a shared multi-touch display.

a color-coded toolbar located on his side of the table (Figure 4.21), into which he can type query terms using a virtual keyboard. The toolbar also contains a *marquee* region, which provides awareness of others' activities by slowly scrolling past color-coded keywords and page titles based on group members' actions. Dragging terms from the marquee onto the search box enables text reuse, in order to reduce typing.

Figure 4.21: Each group member of the WeSearch system has his own color-coded toolbar, into which he can enter queries, either by typing on a virtual keyboard or dragging and dropping text from elsewhere on the display. One such source of reusable text is the marquee, located immediately above the search box, which displays a slowly-scrolling collection of terms and images from group members recent queries and webpage views. In addition to retrieving entire webpages, the "clips" button enables users to retrieve smaller snippets of information, such as images, news articles, or suggested query alternatives, displayed here in piles above the toolbar.

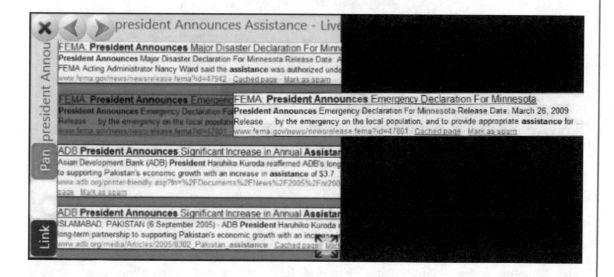

Figure 4.22: Pressing the "clips" button on a WeSearch browser automatically segments a page into chunks such as paragraphs, headings, and images, based on the page's DOM. These clips can be removed from the browser as a means for reducing clutter (by enabling the larger pages to be closed) and for supporting sensemaking (by enabling users to identify the most relevant content within a page).

The WeSearch browser supports automatically dividing a webpage into smaller component pieces, called *clips*, by parsing the DOM (Figure 4.22). This allows individual images and paragraphs to be dragged out of the browser in order to reduce on-screen clutter (by enabling users to close the original pages) and support sensemaking (by enabling users to identify the most relevant content and put it within *containers* (Figure 4.23)). The search-by-example feature analyzes containers' contents

Figure 4.23: Containers provide a place for WeSearch users to organize their clips, in order to facilitate sensemaking; containers providing several different organization templates (such as lists and grids) are available. To reduce the need for textentry on multi-touch surfaces, container contents are analyzed for commonalities, resulting in suggested search terms that appear on the container's bottom border.

for similarities, and it proactively suggests new query terms that might be useful. These suggested queries can be issued without additional typing, by touching the suggestion region. Groups can also export an XML record of their WeSearch session, which contains information about every component clip, including which group member found it and how (i.e., using what keywords), and what container it was organized into. This meta-data rich exported record, viewable in any Web browser, enables individual, post-meeting sensemaking and reflection.

Evaluations of WeSearch found that the marquee feature enhanced awareness of group members' search strategies, promoting conversation, and that clips and containers were successful in supporting sensemaking as an integral part of the search process. Text-reuse and report-exporting features were also highly valued. However, clutter and the use of virtual keyboards remained problematic for users. Advances in tabletop hardware, such as higher resolution displays and tactile feedback for text entry, may be necessary in combination with WeSearch's UI innovations in order to make these devices offer a top-quality search experience.

4.3   WHERE: CONCLUSIONS AND FUTURE DIRECTIONS

Whether users are co-located or remote impacts the types of features that a collaborative search system might need to provide. Features that enable distributed control become important in co-located settings, while features supporting mutual awareness take on heightened importance in remote scenarios. Understanding what combinations of features are best suited to mixed-presence collaborations is still an open research question.

The introduction of devices with new capabilities, such as interactive displays with higher precision touch input, richer integration with tangibles, and higher-resolution output, or mobile phones offering easier connectivity to and control of external devices, offer exciting new possibilities for designing search systems that support a variety of flexible work configurations, in both fixed and on-the-go settings. An open challenge introduced by this increasing ecology of devices is exploring how to design systems that enable collaboration when different group members are using different devices with different capabilities. For example, Martha could have searched with her family in a mixed-presence setting where George and Martha gathered around a tabletop display in their living room, while Beth connected to the search using her personal computer, and Martha's mother called in from the airport via a mobile phone. Wiltse and Nichols (2009) PlayByPlay system, pictured in Figure 4.24, which enables remote collaboration on Web browsing when one user has a mobile phone and the other has a PC, is one example of a step down this largely unexplored research path.

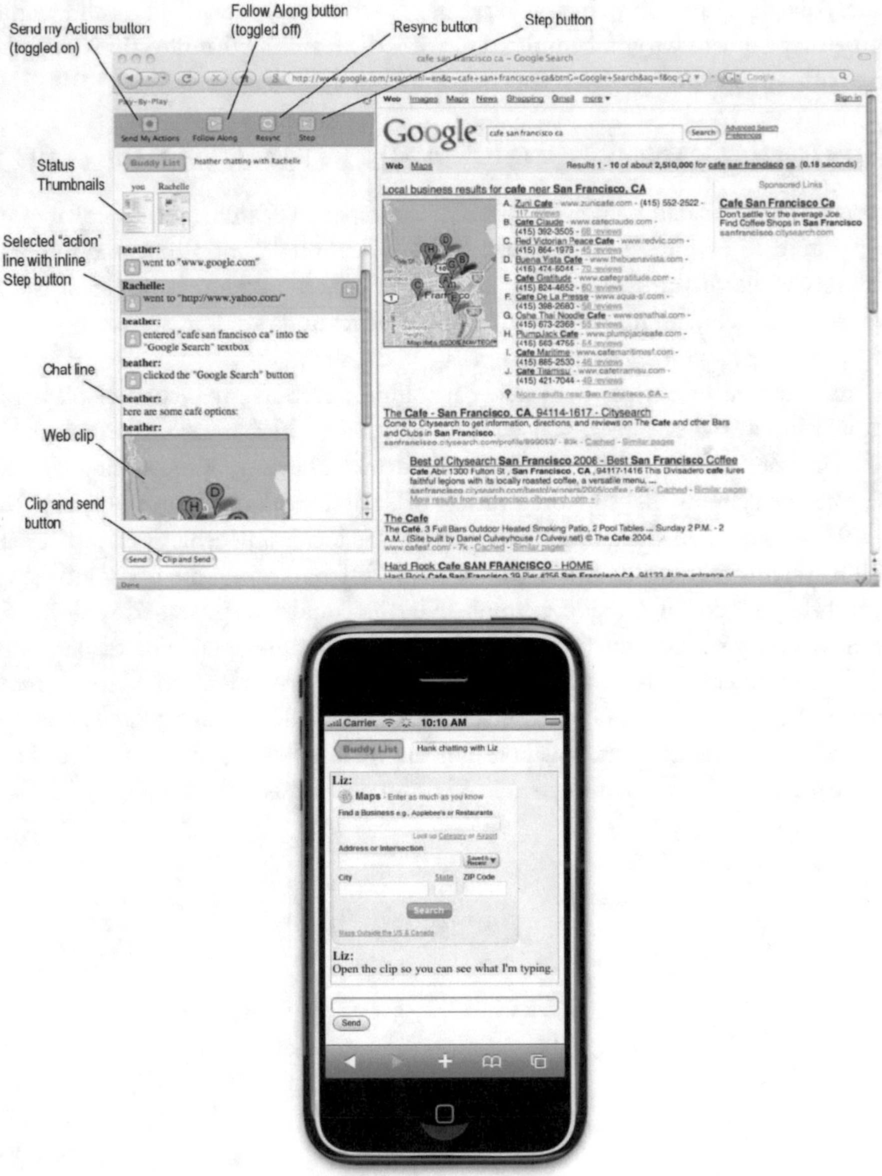

Figure 4.24: PlayByPlay (Wiltse and Nichols, 2009) enables remote collaboration on Web browsing when one user has a mobile phone and the other has a PC, by allowing the user with the more impoverished phone interface to delegate tasks to the PC user, yet remain aware of their actions.

CHAPTER 5

When?

When a group collaborates on a search task, the temporal nature of their collaboration has important implications for the types of algorithmic and user interface features that can best support them. Broadly, there are two main temporal patterns to collaborative work: *asynchronous* and *synchronous*. Synchronous collaboration refers to situations in which all group members are working at the same time, whereas asynchronous collaboration refers to situations in which group members' efforts do not necessarily overlap temporally. In this chapter, we provide an overview of systems designed to support both methods of interaction, and look in-depth at S^3 (Morris and Horvitz, 2007a), which supports asynchronous collaboration, and CoSense (Paul and Morris, 2009), which supports synchronous work.

5.1 ASYNCHRONOUS COLLABORATION

There are many situations in which collaborators work asynchronously on shared search tasks; this is particularly true for tasks that may extend over multiple separate sessions, such as in complex decision-making or research tasks like the one Martha and her family members engaged in. In the absence of specialized support systems for collaborative search, the two primary strategies groups use to coordinate their asynchronous search process are *divide-and-conquer* and *brute force* (Morris, M.R., 2008).

In the divide-and-conquer approach, group members explicitly divide up a task, either according to sub-tasks (e.g., Martha searched for price information for mold removal companies and George for reputation information) or according to aspects of the search process, such as the search sources used (e.g., Martha could have searched for mold removal companies via the Yellow Pages, while George searched an online review site).

In contrast, the brute force approach reflects a lack of explicit division of labor. Group members avoid the overhead of coordinating on their search strategies ahead of time, but they risk realizing they have gathered redundant information when they share their findings. Martha and Beth's collaboration had very low overhead, but it resulted in significant duplication of effort.

E-mailing a list of links to collaborators is the most common means of sharing the products of an asynchronous searching session (Morris, M.R., 2008). Printing paper copies of relevant websites to give to others is another common strategy. More effortful alternatives, such as creating a document or webpage summarizing the findings of a search, are less prevalent. Sharing practices are listed in Table 3.1.

These practices are similar to what researchers have observed people do to keep information they have encountered around for future personal use (Jones et al., 2002). In a way, the keeping of found information is like collaborating with one's future self, with the individual sharing links and information that will help that individual pick the task up later (Morris and Horvitz, 2007a). Martha, for example, could have emailed herself the links she found while searching immediately after receiving her diagnosis that she thought would be useful to her later. As noted by Jones et al. (2002), a number of the methods people use to make things easier to find later actually have social or communication benefits. Although Jones et al. studied diverse keeping methods, such as bookmarking or saving to a file, from a personal re-finding perspective, the authors highlighted emailing information to other people, printing out information, and posting information to a website, all mentioned above, as having additional communication benefits.

The tools designed to help people manage their complex individual search tasks that extend over time include bookmarking, histories, or systems that allow users to flag pages or parts of pages for inclusion in a workspace, such as SearchPad (Bharat, K., 2000) or Hunter Gatherer (Schraefel et al., 2002). These systems allow an individual to collaborate with their past self when they resume a previously begun search task.

Social search systems that allow individuals to take advantage of information from others, but that are non-collaborative, are generally asynchronous in nature. For example, data from a community of related users running searches at earlier times can be used to re-rank search results (e.g., (Smyth, B., 2007; Smyth et al., 2009; Teevan et al., 2009b)). And systems in which a user's question is federated to a social network (e.g., (Evans et al., 2010; Morris et al., 2010c)) tend to receive responses after a period of time has elapsed. Understanding how to manage the trade offs between the speed of responses from traditional search engines and the personalized, high-quality responses returned asynchronously from social sources is an open research problem.

For systems supporting asynchronous active collaboration among users with shared goals, the creation of a persistent artifact representing the current state of the search is important. This artifact may exist as stateful data stored in the cloud (e.g., as in SearchTogether (Morris and Horvitz, 2007b)) so that it can be accessed by group members at any time. Alternately, a file metaphor can be used, enabling sharing of the artifact via traditional mechanisms such as email. S^3 (Morris and Horvitz, 2007a) is an example of a collaborative search system specifically designed to support this style of asynchronous collaboration; we discuss S^3 in more detail in the following section.

5.1.1   EXAMPLE: S^3 (STORABLE, SHAREABLE SEARCH)

The S^3 ("Storable, Shareable Search") system facilitates asynchronous collaborative Web search tasks by adopting a file metaphor. S^3 uses a persistent XML data format (referred to as a .srch file) to represent both the process and products of an ongoing search task. This file can be saved, loaded, edited, and shared in a manner analogous to a word processing document or spreadsheet. The opening, saving, and editing takes place using the special S^3 browser (Figure 5.1). Sharing occurs by sending the resulting .srch file as a simple email attachment.

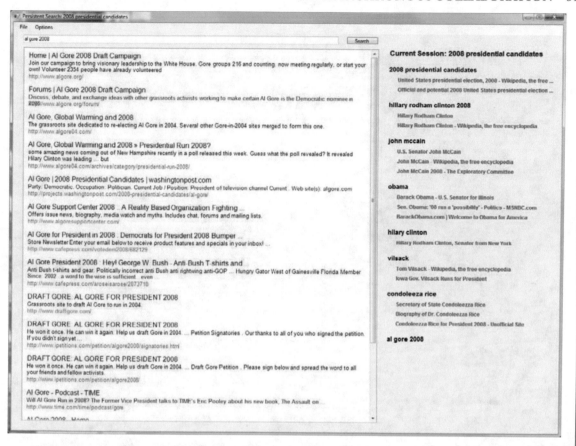

Figure 5.1: S³ (Morris and Horvitz, 2007a) users use a special Web browser that automatically records the state of their search (shown in the session overview on the browsers right-hand side). This state can then be saved (and later loaded) as an XML file.

As the user searches in the S³ browser, the system automatically records all queries entered, results retrieved, and subsequent pages visited. Users can optionally associate comments with particular search results by right-clicking them and choosing the "comment" option from the browser's context menu. A summary of the user's queries and page visits is displayed alongside the browser. Clicking this overview takes the user to the detailed view of the saved search file, which is also the default view one sees upon loading a saved search (Figure when-s3-file).

This detailed view of a saved search file shows each query issued during the search task, in chronological order. Below each query is a list of the associated webpages the user visited. Each page is represented by a detailed entry, including the title, snippet, URL, and thumbnail. An indication of the identity of the user who viewed each page is also shown (to facilitate awareness of the collaborative

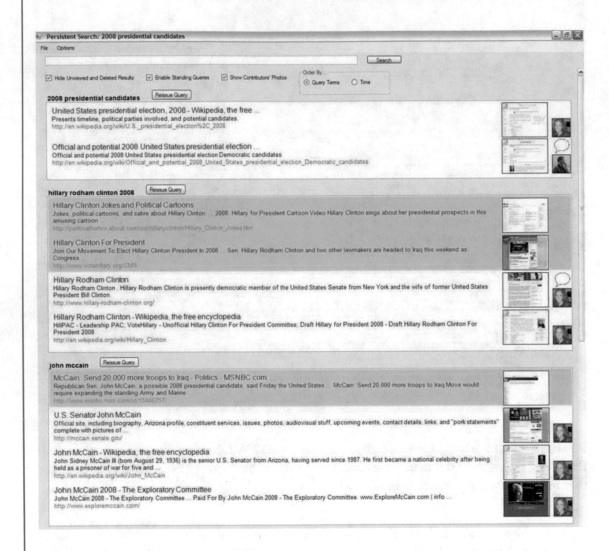

Figure 5.2: Loading a saved search file in S^3 provides a detailed overview of a search's state, including the query terms used and resulting pages visited, the identity of the user who visited each page, and any comments attached to the page. Such files can be sent back and forth as email attachments and sequentially augmented, in order to support asynchronous collaboration. Pages highlighted in green have been proactively fetched by the system as part of its "standing query" feature, to inform the user of new, relevant material that may interest her.

evolution of the search task) as well as an icon indicating whether any comments have been attached to the page; hovering over the comment icon reveals the full text of the comments.

In addition to facilitating asynchronous collaboration, persistently representing a search in this fashion also facilitates informing a user about newly available, relevant content. For example, S^3 provides a *standing queries* feature, which, upon opening a saved search file, reissues its component queries behind-the-scenes, and downloads and highlights newly-available, highly-ranked results for each query. Increasing users' awareness of newly-available Web content has recently become an active area of research, such as the development of change-aware Web browsers (Teevan et al., 2009a). Considering how this type of change awareness could translate to mechanisms for awareness of what Web content one's collaborators have or have not viewed is an interesting area for future work.

5.2   SYNCHRONOUS COLLABORATION

Although it is often convenient to work asynchronously, there are many situations when group members simultaneously approach their shared search task. Scenarios where users are physically co-located generally result in synchronous collaboration, such as when Martha and George at home, colleagues in a meeting, or students in a classroom work together to find information in support of a shared project. Systems designed for co-located collaborative search, therefore, also include features to support synchronous input, such as the input queuing mechanisms of CoSearch (Amershi and Morris, 2008) or the use of specialized multi-input-aware surfaces in systems like WeSearch (Morris et al., 2010b), Cambiera (Isenberg and Fisher, 2009), TeamSearch (Morris et al., 2006), Físchlár-DT (Smeaton et al., 2006), and WebSurface (Tuddenham et al., 2009).

Some synchronous collaboration systems are designed specifically for scenarios where users are working together at the same time, yet they have differing roles in the search process. For example, guided search tools support role-differentiated synchronous searching, such as receiving the assistance of an online reference librarian via QuestionPoint (`http://www.oclc.org/questionpoint`) or of a more experienced searcher via ChaCha (`http://chacha.com`).

For users with shared goals (i.e., one is not merely assisting the other out of professional obligation), specialized synchronous tools have also been developed. For instance, the Smart Splitting tool (Morris et al., 2008) (Figure 2.3) assists with division of labor among groups where members have different areas of expertise, by partitioning a single set of search results among their respective machines based on an adaptation of personalization algorithms. Cerchiamo (Pickens et al., 2008) (Figure 2.1) algorithmically merges input from two users, the "miner" and the "prospector," in real time in order to increase the relevance of video-search results.

Finally, some systems have been designed to support real-time collaboration amongst sets of peers in disparate locations. Although its persistent state enables asynchronous work, SearchTogether (Morris and Horvitz, 2007b) also supports a synchronous collaboration mode, and it provides division of labor features to facilitate that process, such as the ability to divide the results of a single query among multiple users or to federate a search to several specialty search engines and provide different group members with different subsets of results. These division of labor features are designed to take advantage of synchronous searching configurations by parallelizing the search task to improve efficiency.

Awareness-promoting features were another important design consideration for supporting synchronous work in SearchTogether. For instance, enabling real-time discussion through integrated instant messaging supports communication during synchronous tasks and is inspired by survey findings showing that with status quo Web browsing tools people use IM and phone conversations to support synchronous, remote collaboration (Morris, M.R., 2008). SearchTogether's more recent addition of "peek" and "follow" features (`http://research.microsoft.com/searchtogether`) (Figure 5.3) facilitate synchronous collaboration by providing co-browsing abilities, enabling for real-time awareness of collaborators' current focus of attention.

Figure 5.3: The SearchTogether browser (`http://research.microsoft.com/searchtogether`) plug-in iterated on the original design (Morris and Horvitz, 2007b) in response to users' desire for more awareness during synchronous collaboration, by adding the "peek" (A) and "follow" (B) buttons, that enable users to engage in either brief (peek) or extended (follow) co-browsing.

The CoSense system (Paul and Morris, 2009) expanded even further upon SearchTogether's awareness features; in the next section, we explore in detail the awareness features CoSense provides to support synchronous collaborative search and how its features are used differently in synchronous and asynchronous scenarios.

5.2.1   EXAMPLE: COSENSE

CoSense (Paul and Morris, 2009) is an extension to the SearchTogether system that provides enhanced awareness of collaborators' activities in order to facilitate sensemaking, both of the products of a collaborative search and of the collaborative search process itself. CoSense offers four different views of the data from a shared search session: a search strategies view, a timeline view, a chat-centric view, and a workspace view.

The search strategies view, shown in Figure 5.4, provides information about the roles and skills of group members, such as the query terms used, domains visited, amount of activity from each group member, and use of advanced techniques such as special search operators or diverse search engines. The timeline view, shown in Figure 5.5, provides an integrated chronological representation of all the actions of all group members during the search session. The chat-centric view, shown in Figure 5.6, contextualizes instant messaging conversations by enabling users to view the page that was open in a collaborator's browser at the time they sent a particular chat message. Finally, the workspace view, shown in Figure 5.7, allows group members to organize the products of their search, maintain notes about task strategy, and link their search findings to external, non-Web documents (such as spreadsheets or text files).

An evaluation of CoSense illustrated how different types of awareness features were valuable for different temporal phases of collaboration. In particular, the evaluation found that group members working together synchronously needed support in making sense of *how* information was being found (i.e., the search process) and thus, more frequently, made use of the search strategies and chat-centric views to understand what other group members were currently working on. In contrast, users collaborating asynchronously needed support in making sense of *what* had been found (i.e., the search products) and, therefore, more heavily used the timeline and workspace views to explore the webpages that had been discovered.

5.3   WHEN: CONCLUSIONS AND FUTURE DIRECTIONS

Researchers have recognized that synchronous and asynchronous collaboration patterns merit consideration when designing collaborative search systems. As we have seen, they have introduced both interface and algorithmic features to support these different temporal work styles. More in-depth evaluations of these systems, in order to better understand how different temporality in collaborations impacts system use, is an important area of future work. The CoSense evaluation summarized in the previous section is an initial step in this direction. Additionally, understanding the *when* of collaborative search at a more fine-grained level is another open issue, such as understanding the

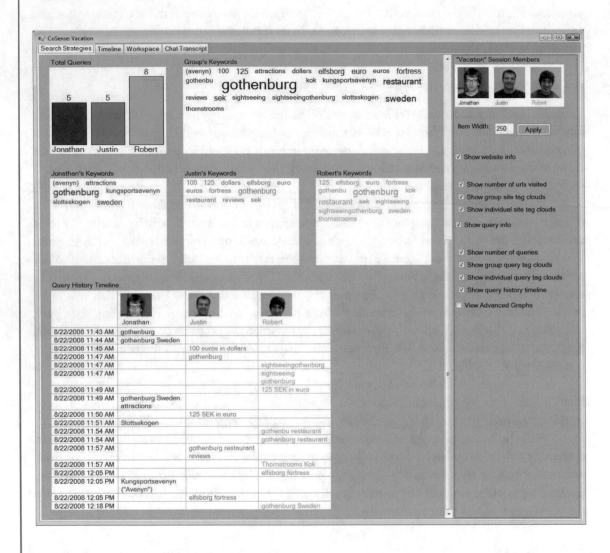

Figure 5.4: CoSense's search strategies view gives an overview of users search processes, including the number, content, and temporal evolution of users' queries, as well as the domains each user subsequently visited. Hovering over search terms or domains in this view's interactive tag clouds provides a list of all of a user's queries that incorporated a term, or all of the sites within a particular domain the user visited; clicking a term opens the sets of search results/websites in multiple browser tabs for exploration. This view was more frequently used during synchronous, rather than asynchronous, collaboration.

Figure 5.5: CoSense's timeline view provides a unified, chronological depiction of a group search session, including all queries executed, webpages visited, comments on pages, and chat messages. This information is color-coded according to user. The timeline can be filtered to show specific activities and/or users, if desired. This view was more frequently used during asynchronous, rather than synchronous, collaboration.

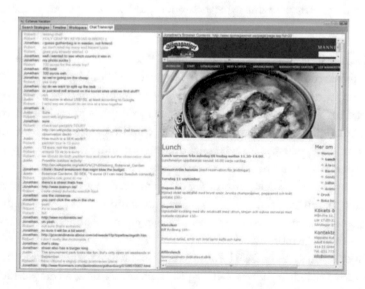

Figure 5.6: CoSense's chat-centric view shows the group's color-coded chat conversation (left). Clicking any chat message shows the webpage that messages author was viewing at the time the message was sent (right). This view was more frequently used during synchronous, rather than asynchronous, collaboration.

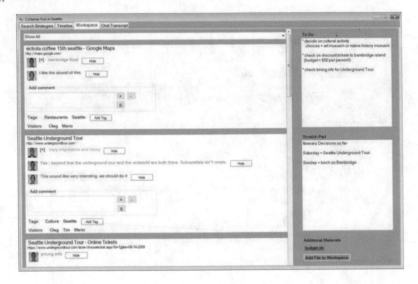

Figure 5.7: CoSense's workspace view depicts the set of webpages that group members have commented on, and allows users to apply tags to organize and make further sense of their findings. These tags can be used to filter the view. The right-hand portion of this view provides free-form "to do" and "scratch pad" lists that can be collaboratively edited, as well as allowing users to link external files to the workspace. This view was more frequently used during asynchronous, rather than synchronous, collaboration.

patterns of tightly-and loosely-coupled collaboration that occur even within a synchronous work session (as some initial studies of TeamSearch (Morris et al., 2006) have begun to do).

Understanding the frequency of users' engagement in collaborative search activities is also an important direction for future work. For instance, if users engage in collaborative search activities very frequently, that might suggest that collaborative search tools should be an integral part of the standard search experience, whereas if such collaborations are more rare, highly-planned events, then dedicated, special-purpose tools might be more appropriate. A diary study of twenty information workers found that over a one-week period they each engaged in an average of two (and maximum of five) collaborative search experiences when using status quo technologies (Amershi and Morris, 2009). Of course, the frequency with which people engage in collaborative searching may increase as the tools to do so become more widespread.

Collaborative search systems may be able to control factors that encourage more active participation in collaborative search activities, helping to transform a slow, asynchronous experience into a faster, more real-time one. For example, research has shown that response times on Q&A sites tend to be long. Zhang et al. (2007) reported that when expert Java users posted questions to the Java Developer Forum, the average time to receive a response was nearly 9 hours. Hsieh and Counts (2009) reported that the average time to receive an answer to a question posted to Microsoft's Live

QnA site was 2 hours and 52 minutes. Hsieh and Counts also reported that 20% of questions posted to Live QnA never received an answer at all. But intrinsic and extrinsic rewards for participating appear to encourage faster, higher quality responses (Raban and Harper, 2008). Even something as simple as how collaborators are portrayed or how information needs are expressed across participants may be important. In the next chapter, we look at why people collaborate on search tasks. This gives us further insight into how we might incentivize faster and more active participation.

CHAPTER 6

Why?

This chapter looks at why people work with the group members they do during collaborative search activities. We begin by looking at how people are brought together because of a shared interest in a common topic, and then we discuss many of the social reasons people might collaborate. We also examine how social search systems that implicitly use groups' data could identify opportunities for transitioning to more explicit collaborations. We conclude with a discussion of how these motivations for collaborating might be supported and enhanced in future collaborative search tools.

6.1 SHARED INTEREST IN A TOPIC

One reason people work together to find information is that they have a shared interest in the topic of the search. For example, because both George and Martha are interested in Martha's health, learning more about asthma and common irritants following her diagnosis was valuable to both of them. There are a number of reasons why turning to other people who share an interest in a topic might benefit the individual, which we examine in this section. We also discuss how existing systems bring together people with common interests, and we suggest ways collaborative search systems might make such topical connections more effectively in the future.

Via a survey of 624 people, Morris et al. (2010c) explored the reasons that people reported for asking and answering questions of people in their online social networks. They found that many of the reasons people reported for answering a question asked by a friend related to the topic of the question being asked. These properties included whether the answerer considered the question's topic interesting, whether the answerer possessed expertise in the question's topic area, and whether the question was scoped to an audience the answerer considered himself part of.

Teevan et al. (2009b) studied the similarity of people with similar interests or long-standing relationships, to understand whether such people engaged in similar tasks, thought the same things were relevant to shared tasks, or had similar user profiles overall. They found that their participants did not have similar profiles or relevance judgments for general search tasks, but that when the tasks related to the topics at the core of users' relationships, they did. For example, coworkers did not find the same things relevant to queries related to photography or restaurants, but did find the same things relevant for topics related to their job.

There are a number of reasons why, when a person shares a topical information need with other people, that person may find it more valuable to satisfy the need with others instead of alone. Table 6.1 lists the most common motivations Morris et al. (2010c) observed for a person to ask their social network a question rather than (or in addition to) conducting a Web search on the topic. They found that some questions' topics were reported as being better suited for discussion among known, trusted people. Groups of people were considered well-suited for answering subjective questions where opinions or recommendations are needed (e.g., Jim's recommendation for a mold inspector is more valuable than a random person's recommendation), questions where a specific group of people know valuable information (e.g., Jim's firsthand experience with mold inspection meant he could suggest good things to watch out for), and for questions where significant existing context could be valuable (e.g., George can better help Martha find a good inspector than others because he knows her sensitivity to price, the importance to her of working with a trustworthy contractor, where her house is located, etc.). Trust in collaborators was the most common motivation Morris et al.'s respondents gave for asking a question to their social network instead of using a search engine, accounting for 24.8% of responses.

Table 6.1: 242 survey respondents (Morris et al., 2010c) described their motivations for posing questions to their online social networks. These motivations can increase our understanding of why users might choose to engage in social and collaborative search activities.

Motivation	Percent	Example Survey Responses
Trust	24.8%	- Because I trust my friends more than I trust strangers. - People that I know are reputable.
Subjective questions	21.5%	- A search engine can provide data but not an opinion. - It has no definite answer, it's more about collecting views rather than finding specific info.
Belief search engine would not work	15.2%	- Because search engine technology doesn't work that well yet. - I'm pretty sure a search engine couldn't answer a question of that nature. - Because search engines don't have breaking news. - Search engines aren't updated often enough.
Specific audience	14.9%	- Friends with kids, first hand real experience. - Better visibility among expert users of SQL Server.
Connect socially	12.4%	- I wanted my friends to be aware that I was asking the question. - I wanted to ask the question but also express my frustration to my social network.
Answer speed	6.6%	- Quick response time, no formalities. - Needed information ASAP.
Context	5.4%	- Friends know my tastes. - Search engine is not personalizable.
Failed search	5.4%	- I tried searching and didn't get good results. - A quick search on the search engine didn't give me any useful results.
Easy	5.4%	- It's easier. Results are targeted…don't need to sift out the 'junk.' - There are too many choices on the Web, I wanted something more filtered. - Didn't want to look through multiple search results for answers.
Answer quality	4.1%	- Human-vetted responses. - Better quality results some of the time.
No harm	3.3%	- No cost.
Fun	2.1%	- More fun.
Non-urgent	1.7%	- I didn't need an answer straight away.

Expertise-finding systems may be useful in helping people find trustworthy collaborators with knowledge of and interest in a particular topic. Expertise-finding systems are systems designed to help users identify people with a particular type of knowledge within a specific organization, social network, or in general. For example, Aardvark (`http://vark.com`) is a commercial expertise-finding system. Users register with Aardvark, tagging themselves with areas of expertise and providing information about their social network. Users then post questions to Aardvark, which are routed to members of their immediate or extended network based on the expertise information. Collabio (Bernstein et al., 2009) is a tagging-based Facebook game designed to augment the social network with metadata that can be used for expertise finding.

Because expertise is a common motivation for answering others' questions, accounting for 31.9% of all answers in the study by Morris et al. (2010c), connecting an individual with an information need with an expert related to that need can sometimes be enough to get the individual's need satisfied. However, a collaborative search/expertise-finding hybrid could augment experts' profiles to include information about their information goals. This would allow people to identify experts with shared goals to collaborate on search tasks.

Another common reported motivation for turning to others rather than searching alone was that a particular topic was ill-suited for individual search using a search engine. Morris et al. (2010c) found that 5.4% of people in their survey reported enlisting the help of their social network to find something after trying to use a search engine on their own and obtaining no results or low-relevance results. They also found that 15.2% of people believed that search engines were fundamentally incapable of answering the categories of questions they were asking, such as questions relating to breaking news or subjective opinions, and so turned to social tools to satisfy their information need without ever attempting to find the information on their own.

In Chapter 3 (*What*), we discussed the common topics people search for collaboratively. Search engines detecting that users are exploring these topics might identify such interactions as opportunities to remind users of collaborative search features in order to create a more satisfying experience. Some topics that are challenging to investigate with search engines might be particularly ripe for a combination of search and social approaches, such as cases where information resources may not be instantiated online (as in Jim's recommendation for a particular mold inspector).

Combining social information with traditional Web search can also potentially broaden a searcher's initially (perhaps overly) narrow definition of the search topic; Indeed, combining multiple users' perspectives on how to approach a particular topic can be one of the benefits of collaborative searching, increasing users' coverage of the information space by combining their different information-seeking strategies, and perhaps ultimately improving their individual search skills through increased exposure to the approaches other users take to investigating a topic (Morris, M.R., 2007).

6.2   SHARED SOCIAL INTERESTS

There are also a number of social reasons people work together on search tasks. In Morris et al. (2010c) study, several people described the act of asking others for help answering a question as "fun." People also reported asking questions of others so that members of their network would be aware of their interests, enabling them to simultaneously satisfy both an information need and a social purpose. The desire to connect socially with others also prompted people when responding to questions, in order to rekindle old friendships, maintain current ones, and create new ones (Table 6.2). Many people were motivated to answer questions because they had free time; in these cases, they would answer if the question was quick to reply to, and because it entertained them to do so.

In addition to providing a fun and socially-connecting experience, involving others in the search process can potentially increase users' confidence that they have found accurate, relevant information (Morris, M.R., 2007). This increase in confidence may be due to having multiple people viewing and confirming the validity of data, or to the increased coverage of the information space resulting from combining multiple users' search strategies; it may also be due to the high level of trust that users place in information provided by friends, family, and colleagues. The most common reason Morris et al. (2010c) participants reported for seeking information via social networks, rather than via a search engine, was that they had more trust in the responses provided by friends. This suggests that helping people identify trustworthy collaborators could be important for initiating collaborative search groups. One way trustworthy collaborators can be identified is via long standing relationships. Martha, for example, relies on her husband, her sister, and a colleague at work to help her find information related to her asthma. The nature of the relationship between collaborators is an important motivator, with people more likely to provide answers to questions posed by closer friends (Morris et al., 2010c).

In addition to fun, connectedness, and trust, another social motivator for working with others on a search can be earning social rewards for such interactions. For example, Morris et al. (2010c) found that some people were motivated to answer other users' questions on social networking sites by a feeling that they were earning social capital, i.e., if they answered others' questions, their own might be more likely to receive replies in the future. Similarly, some answered out of a feeling of obligation, because they had received help in the past or because they felt indebted to a particular community (Morris et al., 2010c).

The mode of collaboration for searches may affect the social benefits and costs of participating, and thus may in turn affect whether people do it. Those who value the social interaction would probably benefit from direct communication between participants as opposed to the abstraction of information. Many people in Morris et al. (2010c) study indicated they would prefer a face-to-face or personal request when answering questions, and they ignored questions directed broadly to the network-at-large, as indicated by comments like, "I would rather be asked directly," and, "My lack of response is motivated by the impersonal nature of the questions."

Some people like to be recognized for how they contribute to a social search. This information could be reflected internally, within a collaborative search tool, or pushed externally for others to

Table 6.2: 408 survey respondents (Morris et al., 2010c) described factors that motivated them to answer questions posed by members of their online social networks. Understanding these motivations might help in the design of incentive systems for collaborative search tools, or in selecting appropriate situations for suggesting serendipitous collaboration opportunities among friends or strangers.

Motivation	Percent	Example Survey Responses
Altruism	37.0%	- Just trying to be helpful. - Being friendly. - Social goodness.
Expertise	31.9%	- If I'm an expert in the area. - [It depends on] my knowledge of the subject that the question refers to.
Properties of question	15.4%	- Interest in the topic. - [If] it is …time sensitive. - Is it directed at me?
Nature of relationship	13.7%	- If I know and like the person. - If I know the person well
Connect socially	13.5%	- Connect with others. - Keeps my network alive.
Free time	12.3%	- Boredom/procrastination. - It's fun to answer.
Social capital	10.5%	- Favor marketplace. - It creates social currency. - I will get help when I need it myself.
Obligation	5.4%	- A tit-for-tat. - It's part of being in a community of trusted people.
Humor	3.7%	- Thinking I might have a witty response.
Ego	3.4%	- Being wanted. - Looking good. - Wish to seem knowledgeable.

view. By looking at what motivates people to ask and answer questions of online communities in general, we can get an idea of the types of rewards that might encourage people to participate fully in collaborative searches. Venues such as electronic bulletin boards, newsgroups, and question-answering sites enable users to post questions targeted either at a particular community or to the world at large. We will refer to the class of sites where users post questions to be answered by a set of users whom they do not know personally as *Q&A sites*.

Some researchers have explored the factors affecting answer quality on Q&A sites. Raban and Harper (2008) point out that a mixture of both intrinsic factors (e.g., perceived ownership of information, gratitude) and extrinsic factors (e.g., reputation systems, monetary payments) motivate Q&A site users to answer questions. Ackerman and Palen (1996) and Beenan et al. (2004) confirmed that intrinsic motivations, such as visibility of expertise and the feeling of making a unique contribution, influence participation in such systems. Results regarding extrinsic motivators have been more mixed – Hsieh and Counts (2009) found that market-based incentives did not increase answer speed or high-quality answers, but Harper et al. (2008) found that fee-based sites produced higher quality answers than free sites. These insights into how social motivations influence system participation suggest that perhaps collaborative search systems might include such mechanisms, such as a "search reputation system" reflecting either a user's general search skills or domain-specific expertise; such reputation mechanisms could also be valuable in helping users identify potential collaborators.

6.3   INTRODUCING POTENTIAL COLLABORATORS

People sometimes receive the assistance of others who share their tasks without the knowledge of either the person providing or receiving the assistance. For example, the clicks Martha made following her search for "asthma causes" may feed back into the ranking algorithm and result in a better result list for someone else searching on asthma causes. Although this implicit collaboration does not fit the definition of collaborative search, there is an opportunity for systems to automatically detect when people have similar needs and introduce them serendipitously so that they can choose to form a more active collaboration if they so desire. For example, question answering websites and message boards often serve to create connections between people with shared interests, which could then lead to future collaborative searches. Serendipitous groupings appear to be common in collaborative search. In a diary study in which information workers recorded their collaborative search experiences over a one-week period, Amershi and Morris (2009) found that the majority of such collaborations (61.9%) were spontaneous, rather than planned.

Collaborative filtering is one way that data from similar people is identified for implicit use in improving the search experience for an individual. As an example, Sugiyama et al. (2004) filled in sparse user term-weight profiles by applying collaborative filtering techniques to provide term weights based on those of users with similar profiles. Sun et al.'s CubeSVD approach (Sun et al., 2005) used click-through data (represented as a user+query+URL triple) to generate personalized Web rankings; they used collaborative filtering techniques to generate missing click-through triples, thereby enhancing their technique's performance. Dou et al. (2007) compared several personalization strategies and found that the use of click-through data and k-nearest neighbor collaborative filtering was a promising approach. Almeida and Almeida (2004) used Bayesian algorithms to cluster users of an online bookstore's search service into communities based on links clicked within the site, and they found that the popularity of different links within different communities could be used to customize search result rankings. VisSearch (Lee and Y-J., 2005) uses data mining to uncover patterns in users' queries and browsing in order to generate recommendations for users with similar queries. Some recommender systems, such as the movie recommender system PolyLens (O'Conner et al., 2001), attempt to generate recommendation lists for groups of users.

Smyth, B. (2007) suggested that click-through data from users in the same "search community" (e.g., a group of people who use a special-interest Web portal or who work at the same company) could enhance search result lists. Smyth provided evidence for the existence of search communities by showing that a group of employees from a single company had a higher query similarity threshold than general Web users. Freyne and Smyth's I-SPY system (Freyne and Smyth, 2006) expanded the notion of search communities to include related communities, measuring intercommunity similarity based on the degree to which communities' queries and result click through overlap. Mei and Church (2008) found that geographic location might serve as a reasonable proxy for community since they observed that grouping users into classes based on the similarity of their IP addresses could improve search results.

In all of the above cases, in addition to merely using data from other people to generate recommendations, these implicit social-searching algorithms could provide a bridge to forming more active collaborative partnerships. For example, group membership could be made explicit and searchers could opt to actively work together on their shared task rather than merely passively contributing their information. Analyzing query logs to determine when users may be simultaneously engaged in related search tasks could be a way to help users form valuable collaborative relationships (Teevan et al., 2009b). Such systems for serendipitously suggesting collaborative search partners could also benefit from infrastructures provided by social Web browsing tools, such as the Sociable Web (Donath and Robertson, 1994) or Community Bar (http://www.communitybar.net/), which allow users to chat with other people who are simultaneously viewing the same webpage.

When groups are explicitly brought together, there may also be the opportunity to use the implicitly captured information they contribute to improve the search experience. Research on personalizing search results (Dou et al., 2007; Smyth, B., 2007; Teevan et al., 2005) has found that implicitly gathered information such as browser history, query history, and desktop information, can be used to improve the ranking of search results on a per-user basis. Teevan et al. (2005) found that the performance of the personalization algorithm they studied improved as more data became available about the target user. This finding suggests that additional data from similar people may be useful in enhancing personalization systems. A collaborative search system could evaluate various metrics behind the scenes, including how similar previously viewed content is, to determine how likely an explicit collaboration is to be of benefit to a particular implicit group were it to decide to suggest it. Teevan et al. (2009b) explored several ways to identify the value of group data, finding that *groupization* (adapting personalization algorithms to incorporate data from a group of users) could yield improved relevance in search result rankings. The improvement yielded by groupization was dependent on aspects of the users' relationships to each other and on their current task. By automatically identifying situations in which methods such as groupization would yield substantial relevance improvements, systems might also be identifying situations in which it would be valuable to suggest more explicit collaborations among that user group.

Of course, privacy concerns are important when automatically bringing together or suggesting collaborators. It may be that for personal or sensitive topics collaboration should not be suggested, or care should be taken to ensure the collaboration is anonymous or with people far outside the searcher's social sphere. Morris et al. (2010c) asked participants to describe why they would choose *not* to answer status-message questions. Many people indicated private topics were a demotivator, although some indicated that they might respond privately to such inquiries. This suggests systems intended to support collaborative search over personal topics should be clear about how information is shared and with whom. Some topics in particular that may be considered too private for suggesting collaborations with previously-unknown users or with users having certain types of relationships such as professional ties, include religion, politics, sex and dating, personal details about friends or family, money, and health (Morris et al., 2010c).

6.4   WHY: CONCLUSIONS AND FUTURE DIRECTIONS

Future collaborative search tools can benefit greatly from understanding why people collaborate. We explored several reasons why people engage with others beyond situations in which they are already explicitly cooperating on a shared task. People also turn to social resources when such sources broadly share their interests in a topic or have special knowledge of a topic, as well as when a topic is challenging to address through traditional Web search. Social motivators, including a desire to connect with others, trust, fun, and reward systems also incent group information-seeking activities.

Identifying when users are investigating a topic well-suited to collaboration and considering how implicit social search techniques like collaborative filtering, search communities, or groupization might be useful for identifying groups of people who could benefit from more explicit collaborations are intriguing areas for future research. Such systems might help users form new collaborations by identifying trustworthy friends, experts, or even unknown people with similar interests. Understanding how such systems might preserve privacy, as well as the role that social rewards and reputation systems might play to incentivize engagement, is a rich area for further exploration.

CHAPTER 7

Conclusion: How?

In this lecture, we have defined the phenomenon of *collaborative search*, i.e., when a group of users work together on a shared information-seeking goal. We first explored *who* engages in collaborative search, discussing specific user populations, group composition, and roles users take on within such groups. Next, we considered *what* tasks motivate such collaborations, and we delved into the structure of such tasks to better understand the appropriate collaborative opportunities at various task stages. We then considered *where* group members are located with respect to each other during such collaborations, as co-located and remote configurations each present unique challenges. We also reflected on *when* such collaborations occur as the temporal nature of group members' activities, either synchronous or asynchronous, impacts users' needs. Lastly, we examined *why* group memberships arise, and we noted that in addition to groups formed explicitly around a shared information need, factors such as general interest in a topic or the desire to connect socially can also motivate group information-seeking behavior, and that opportunities exist for transforming implicitly formed groups into more explicit collaborators.

Armed with an understanding of the *who*, *what*, *where*, *when*, and *why* of collaborative search, we turn to the question of *how* collaborative search systems can evolve from research prototypes to mainstream adoption. Our discussion of who collaborates on search and what tasks motivate joint information-seeking has established that there is real need and motivation from end-users for improved social features in search tools, and our investigation of why groups form indicates that combining the data from and efforts of a group of people can enhance system and user performance on information retrieval tasks. Such findings, combined with the recent popularity of online social tools such as Facebook (http://facebook.com) and Twitter (http://twitter.com), suggest that both end-users and commercial entities have motivation to evolve browsers and search engine functionality from single-user scenarios to collaborative ones. Indeed, recent announcements by major search companies (Mayer, M., 2009; Microsoft, 2009) suggest that such changes are on the near-term horizon.

As a research community, how can we speed up the mainstream adoption of collaborative search tools and assure that such tools meet their full potential? In the concluding section of each chapter in this lecture, we identified areas for future work. Pursuing those themes is a key next step for advancing the state of the art and the state of our understanding. Collaboration among several communities is key to such advancements. In particular, experts from the library sciences, information retrieval specialists, and user interface researchers can combine their skills to better understand collaborative information seeking scenarios, create and refine algorithms and interfaces to support those needs, and evaluate the impact of the resulting innovations.

7.1   SCENARIO: COLLABORATION TOMORROW

We conclude by revisiting Martha's scenario from the Introduction, envisioning how her search might have progressed if she had access to some of the emerging technologies discussed throughout this lecture.

At her doctor's appointment, Martha learns that her recent breathing difficulties have been caused by asthma. Martha's doctor prescribes some steroid medications to ease her breathing, and using the computer in the exam room, augments Martha's electronic health record with a medical search stub containing links to trusted websites describing the medication, as well as medical terminology used during the appointment that Martha had asked him to define for her. When Martha returns to her office, she logs into her health record and uses the search terms and sites her doctor entered there as a jumping-off point to learn more about the treatments he prescribed, as well as the factors that might have contributed to her adult-onset asthma.

Martha's search yields several results claiming to list causes of and treatments for asthma, but she is able to choose which to explore in-depth because her browser shows her which results come from domains that were rated as trusted by her physician. One of these sites mentions that environmental factors can be an asthma trigger, and it lists several common household irritants. She wants to share this list with her husband, who isn't online at the moment, so she uses the browser's "share" feature and selects her husband's identity from her contacts list.

When Martha returns home, she tells her husband, George, about her desire to check whether their home contains any of the irritants she learned about online. They turn on their family computer, and when George opens the browser he can see that Martha has shared a webpage with him; clicking the notification opens the list of household irritants in his browser. George scrolls through the article quickly, so Martha opens her mobile phone browser and tells it to synch to the nearest PC, enabling her to view the same content as George, but to read it at her own pace. As George and Martha each read through the list, they annotate the webpage to indicate which items they know don't apply to their home; their annotations are synched across their devices in real time, and soon they can see that the only irritant neither of them can confirm is not present in their home is mold.

George begins searching for information on local mold-inspection companies. Martha receives a phone call from her sister, Beth, so she exits the session in order to take the call, but knows it will be easy for her to see George's queries and findings the next time she logs into her browser. Martha discusses her diagnosis with Beth. Since Beth is concerned about her condition, Martha adds Beth to the list of people who can access her search materials on asthma. After their phone conversation, Beth reviews the materials from Martha's search, and she sees that Martha and George are considering mold-removal as a preventative treatment option. Beth recalls that her friend Jim, who lives near Martha, considered using a mold-removal service last year, and she sends a note to Jim asking him whether he has any information that could help Martha and George select a reliable company.

Although it's been a year since Jim conducted his search, he is able to check his browser's topical search-session history to return to the collection of queries and pages he used in making his choice. His search includes comments he added to several companies' sites containing pricing information that he gathered in a time-consuming process by speaking to representatives from each service, as well as reputation information for several companies that he obtained by asking his online social network for their feedback on this issue. He shares this information with Martha and George, so that they don't need to spend hours re-visiting this same process themselves. Using Jim's data, Martha and George select a contractor to remove the mold from their home, hopeful that it will relieve Martha's symptoms.

Glossary

asymmetric collaboration A collaboration in which the collaborators fulfill different roles. This may arise as a result of a division of a search task into roles based on familiarity with technology, job hierarchy, or specific expertise. It also can arise as a result of asymmetric information needs, where one collaborator enlists the assistance of others. Examples of this include receiving assistance from a reference librarian, participating in a guided search experience, or querying a social network. (See also **symmetric collaboration**.)

asynchronous collaboration Collaborations in which group members' efforts do not necessarily overlap temporally. (See also **synchronous collaboration**.)

awareness Real-time awareness of collaborators' current focus of attention is sometimes important for collaboration, and many collaborative search tools have features designed to support such awareness. (See also **division of labor** and **persistence**.)

brute force The brute force approach to collaborative search reflects a lack of explicit division of labor. Group members avoid the overhead of coordinating on their search strategies ahead of time but risk realizing they have gathered redundant information when they share their findings. (See also **divide-and-conquer**.)

collaborative search The subset of social search where several users share an information need, and actively work together to fulfill that need.

co-located collaboration A collaboration where collaborators are physically co-present. (See also **remote collaboration** and **mixed-presence collaboration**.)

division of labor The division of the effort involved in a collaborative search among collaborators is sometimes an important feature of collaboration, and many collaborative search tools have features designed to support such division. (See also **awareness** and **persistence**.)

divide-and-conquer Group members explicitly divide up a task, either according to sub-tasks (e.g., one spouse searches for information on asthma treatments and another for information on asthma irritants) or according to aspects of the search process, such as the search sources used (e.g., one spouse searches for contractors to remove mold via a yellow pages search engine and another searches on a review site). (See also **brute force**.)

exploratory search A search carried out by searchers who are unfamiliar with the domain of their goal, unsure of how to achieve their goal, or unsure of what their goal is. It includes a broad class of activities, such as investigating, comparing, and synthesizing information related to the goal.

information goal The information a person is looking for during a search. (See also **information target**.)

information target The information a person is looking for during a search (see also **information goal**).

informational intent A search intended to find a piece of information. (See also **navigational intent** and **transactional intent**.)

keyword search A search conducted by issuing a keyword query to a search engine.

mixed-presence collaboration A collaboration in which a subset of the group is co-located, while others are remote. (See also **co-located collaboration** and **remote collaboration**.)

navigational intent A search intended to find a particular resource. (See also **informational intent** and **transactional intent**.)

orienteer The process of finding an information target using clues from the information environment . (See also **teleport**.)

persistence Having information about the process and product of a search persist across search sessions is sometimes important for collaboration, and many collaborative search tools have features designed to support persistence. (See also **awareness** and **division of labor**.)

process-related collaboration One place that collaboration can occur is in the search process. In process-related collaboration, group members collaborate on how to find information. (See also **product-related collaboration**.)

product-related collaboration One place that collaboration can occur is over the products (i.e., findings) of a search. In product-related collaboration, group members can collaborate by exchanging the sought-after information with one another. (See also **process-related collaboration**.)

remote collaboration A collaboration where collaborators are in distinct locations. (See also **co-located collaboration** and **mixed-presence collaboration**.)

search engine A search tool that supports keyword search. Given a query, a search engine returns a ranked list of related documents.

sensemaking The process of finding meaning in a situation; in particular, the cognitive act of understanding the information found via a search.

social search Social search refers broadly to the process of finding information online with the assistance of social resources. For example, most commercial search engines use some social resources to improve the search experience through re-ranking or keyword suggestions. Other social search behaviors include asking other people for assistance with a search or conducting a search over an existing database of social content (e.g., public Twitter postings).

strategy A plan for how the searcher will go about finding the information that is being sought. Process-related collaboration and product-related collaboration are examples of collaborative search strategies. (See also **tactic**.)

symmetric collaboration A collaboration in which the collaborators share an information need and fulfill the same roles. (See also **asymmetric collaboration**.)

synchronous collaboration Synchronous collaboration refers to situations in which all group members work at the same time. (See also **asynchronous collaboration**.)

tactic A specific action that assists a user in implementing a search strategy. Keyword search is a common search tactic. (See also **strategy**.)

teleport A search strategy intended to jump directly to an information target by describing the target fully up front. (See also **orienteer**.)

transactional intent A search intended to perform some action, such as paying bills. (See also **informational intent** and **navigational intent**.)

Web search The process of finding information on the World Wide Web. Web search refers both to the process of entering keywords into an online search engine and the related ecology of online information-seeking activities, such as browsing to specific URLs, making sense of found content, iteratively revising a query, and disseminating results.

Bibliography

Ackerman, M. and Malone, T. (1990) Answer Garden: A Tool for Growing Organizational Memory. *Proceedings of SIGOIS 1990*, 31-39. DOI: 10.1145/91474.91485 1.1, 1.3.5

Ackerman, M. and Palen, L. (1996) The Zephyr Help Instance: Promoting Ongoing Activity in a CSCW System. *Proceedings of CHI 1996*, 268-275. DOI: 10.1145/238386.238528 6.2

Almeida, R. and Almeida, V. (2004) A Community-Aware Search Engine. *Proceedings of WWW 2004*, 413-421. DOI: 10.1145/988672.988728 6.3

Amershi, S. and Morris, M.R. (2008) CoSearch: A System for Co-located Collaborative Web Search. *Proceedings of CHI 2008*, 1647-1656. DOI: 10.1145/1357054.1357311 1.2, 1.3.3, 2.1, 2.2, 2.3, 3.1, 3.1, 4.2, 4.2.1, 4.17, 4.2, 5.2

Amershi, S. and Morris, M.R. (2009) Co-located Collaborative Web Search: Understanding Status Quo Practices. *Proceedings of CHI 2009 Extended Abstracts*. DOI: 10.1145/1520340.1520547 2.1, 2.3, 4.2, 5.3, 6.3

Amershi, S., Morris, M.R., Moraveji, N., Balakrishnan, R., and Toyoma, K. (2010) Multiple Mouse Text Entry for Single-Display Groupware. *Proceedings of CSCW 2010*, in press. 4.2.1

Bates, M.J. (1979a) Idea Tactics. *Journal of the American Society for Information Science*, 30(5), 281-289. DOI: 10.1002/asi.4630300507 3.2, 3.3

Bates, M.J. (1979b) Information Search Tactics. *Journal of the American Society for Information Science*, 30(4), 205-214. 3.2, 3.3

Beenan, G., Ling, K., Wang, X., Chang, K., Frankowski, D., Resnick, P., and Kraut, R.E. (2004) Using Social Psychology to Motivate Contributions to Online Communities. *Proceedings of CSCW 2004*, 212-221. DOI: 10.1145/1031607.1031642 6.2

Beitzel, S.M., Jensen, E.C., Chowdhury, A., Grossman, D., and Frieder, O. (2004) Hourly analysis of a very large topically categorized Web query log. *Proceedings of SIGIR 2004*, 321-328. DOI: 10.1145/1008992.1009048 3.1

Bernstein, M., Tan, D., Smith, G., Czerwinski, M., and Horvitz, E. (2009) Collabio: A Game for Annotating People within Social Networks. *Proceedings of UIST 2009*, 97-100. 1.3.5, 6.1

Bharat, K. (2000) SearchPad: Explicit Capture of Search Context to Support Web Search. *Proceedings of WWW 2000*, 493-501. DOI: 10.1016/S1389-1286(00)00047-5 5.1

Blackwell, A., Stringer, M., Toye, E., and Rode, J. (2004) Tangible Interface for Collaborative Information Retrieval. *Proceedings of CHI 2004*, 1473-1476. DOI: 10.1145/985921.986093 4.2, 4.10

Broder, A. (2002) A Taxonomy of Web Search. *ACM SIGIR Forum*, 36(2), 2002, 3-10. DOI: 10.1145/792550.792552 3.1

Bruce, H., Fidel, R., Pejtersen, A.M., Dumais, S.T., Grudin, J., and Poltrock, S. (2002) A Comparison of Collaborative Information Retrieval (CIR) Behaviors of Two Design Teams. In *Information Seeking in Context*, 2002. 3.2

Cabri, G., Leonardi, L., and Zambonelli, F. (1999) Supporting Cooperative WWW Browsing: A Proxy-Based Approach. *Seventh Euromicro Workshop on Parallel and Distributed Processing*, 1999, 138-145. DOI: 10.1109/EMPDP.1999.746657 4.1

Cao, H., Jiang, D., Pei, J., He, Q., Liao, Z., Chen, E., and Li, H. (2008) Context-Aware Query Suggestion by Mining Click-Through and Session Data. *Proceedings of SIGKDD*, 2008, 875-883. DOI: 10.1145/1401890.1401995 1.1

Donath, J. and Robertson, N. (1994) The Sociable Web. *Second International WWW Conference*, 1994. 4.1, 6.3

Dou, Z., Song, R. and Wen, J. R. (2007) A Large-Scale Evaluation and Analysis of Personalized Search Strategies. *Proceedings of WWW 2007*, 581-590. DOI: 10.1145/1242572.1242651 6.3

Evans, B. and Chi, E. (2008) Towards a Model of Understanding Social Search. *Proceedings of CSCW 2008*, 485-494. DOI: 10.1145/1460563.1460641 1.1, 2.1, 3.2, 3.1, 3.7, 3.3

Evans, B., Kairam, S., and Pirolli, P. (2010) Do Your Friends Make You Smarter? An Analysis of Social Strategies in Online Information Seeking. *Information Processing and Management*, in press. 2.2, 5.1

Fallows, D. (2008) Search Engine Use. *Pew Internet and American Life Project*. August 6, 2008. 1

Fidel, R., Bruce, H., Peitersen, A., Dumais, S., Grudin, J., and Poltrock, S. (2000) Collaborative Information Retrieval. *Review of Information Behavior Research*, 1(1), 2000, 235-247. 2.1

Freyne, J. and Smyth, B. (2006) Cooperating Search Communities. *Proceedings of AH 2006*, 101-110. 2.2, 6.3

Gianoutsos, S. and Grundy, J. (1996) Collaborative Work with the World Wide Web: Adding CSCW Support to a Web Browser. *Proceedings of OZ-CSCW 1996*, 14-21. 4.1

Gilbert, E. and Karahalios, K. (2009) Predicting Tie Strength with Social Media. *Proceedings of CHI 2009*, 211-220. DOI: 10.1145/1518701.1518736 2.2

Greenberg, S. and Roseman, M. (1996) GroupWeb: A WWW Browser as Real Time Groupware. *Proceedings of CHI 1996 Conference Companion.* 4.1

Hansen, P., and Jarvelin, K. (2005) Collaborative Information Retrieval in an Information-Intensive Domain. *Information Processing and Management*, 41(5), 2005, 1101-1119. DOI: 10.1016/j.ipm.2004.04.016 2.3

Harper, F.M., Raban, D., Rafaeli, S., and Konstan, J.A. (2008) Predictors of Answer Quality in Online Q&A Sites. *Proceedings of CHI 2008*, 865-874. DOI: 10.1145/1357054.1357191 6.2

Hartmann, B., Morris, M.R., Benko, H., and Wilson, A. (2009) Augmenting Interactive Tables with Mice & Keyboards. *Proceedings of UIST 2009*, 149-152. DOI: 10.1145/1622176.1622204 4.2

Hoppe, H.U. and Zhao, J. (1994) C-TORI: An Interface for Cooperative Database Retrieval. *Proceedings of the 5th International Conference on Database and Expert Systems Applications*, 103-113, 1994. DOI: 10.1007/3-540-58435-8_175 1.3.4, 4.1

Hsieh, G. and Counts, S. (2009) mimir: A Market-Based Real-Time Question and Answer Service. *Proceedings of CHI 2009*, 769-778. 5.3, 6.2

Isenberg, P. and Fisher, D. (2009) Collaborative Brushing and Linking for Co-located Visual Analytics of Document Collections. *Proceedings of Eurographics/IEEE-VGTC Symposium on Visualization (EuroViz 2009)*, 1031-1038. DOI: 10.1111/j.1467-8659.2009.01444.x 4.2, 4.14, 5.2

Joachims, T. (2002) Optimizing Search Engines Using Clickthrough Cata. *Proceedings of SIGKDD 2002*, 133-142. 1.1, 1.3.5

Jones, W., Dumais, S.T., and Bruce, H. (2002) Once Found, What Then? A Study of "Keeping" Behaviors in Personal Use of Web Information. *Proceedings of ASIST 2002*, 391-402. 5.1

Jones, R., Rey, B., Madani, O., and Greiner, W. (2006) Generating Query Substitutions. *Proceedings of WWW 2006*, 387-396. DOI: 10.1002/meet.1450390143 1.1

Keller, R., Wolf, S., Chen, J., Rabinowitz, J., and Mathe, N. (1997) A Bookmarking Service for Organizing and Sharing URLs. *Proceedings of WWW 1997*, 1103-1114. DOI: 10.1145/1135777.1135835 4.1

Kleinberg, J.M. (1999) Authoritative sources in a hyperlinked environment. *Journal of the ACM*, 46(5), 1999, 604-632. 1.1, 1.3.5

Krishnappa, R. (2005) Multi-User Search Engine: Supporting Collaborative Information Seeking and Retrieval. *Master's Thesis, University of Missouri-Rolla*, 2005. DOI: 10.1145/324133.324140 1.3.4, 4.1

Large, A., Beheshti, J., and Rahman, T. (2002) Gender Differences in Collaborative Web Searching Behavior: An Elementary School Study. *Information Processing and Management*, 38(3), 2002, 427-443. 2.1, 3.1

Lee, Y-J. (2005) VizSearch: A Collaborative Web Searching Environment. *Computers & Education*, 44(4), 2005, 423-439. DOI: 10.1016/S0306-4573(01)00034-6 6.3

Maekawa, T., Hara, T., and Nishio, S. (2006) A Collaborative Web Browsing System for Multiple Mobile Users. *Proceedings of PERCOM 2006*, 22-35. DOI: 10.1016/j.compedu.2004.04.009 4.2, 4.9

Mayer, M. (2009) Tweets and Updates and Search, Oh My! *The Official Google Blog*, October 21,2009, `http://googleblog.blogspot.com/2009/10/ rt-google-tweets-and-updates-and-search.html` DOI: 10.1109/PERCOM.2006.1 7

Mei, Q. and Church, K. (2008) Entropy of Search Logs: How Hard is Search? With Personalization? With Backoff? *Proceedings of WSDM 2008*, 45-54. 6.3

Microsoft. (2009) Share Your Search with Bing and Ping. *Bing Blog*, September 3, 2009, `http://www.bing.com/community/blogs/search/archive/2009/09/03/ share-your-search-with-bing-and-ping.aspx` DOI: 10.1145/1341531.1341540 7

Morris, M.R., Paepcke, A., and Winograd, T. (2006) TeamSearch: Comparing Techniques for Co-Present Collaborative Search of Digital Media. *Proceedings of Tabletop 2006*, 97-104. DOI: 10.1109/tabletop.2006.32 1.3.4, 4.2, 4.13, 5.2, 5.3

Morris, M.R. (2007) Interfaces for Collaborative Exploratory Web Search: Motivations and Directions for Multi-User Designs. *CHI 2007 Workshop on Exploratory Search and HCI*, 2007. DOI: 10.1109/TABLETOP.2006.32 1, 6.1, 6.2

Morris, M.R. (2008) A Survey of Collaborative Web Search Practices. *Proceedings of CHI 2008*, 1657–1660. 1, 1.2, 2.1, 2.2, 3.1, 3.1, 3.2, 3.2, 3.3, 4.1, 4.2, 5.1, 5.2

Morris, M.R. and Horvitz, E. (2007a) S^3: Storable, Shareable Search. *Proceedings of Interact 2007*, 120–123. 1.3.4, 4.1, 5, 5.1, 5.1

Morris, M.R. and Horvitz, E. (2007b) SearchTogether: An Interface for Collaborative Web Search. *Proceedings of UIST 2007*, 3-12. 1.3.3, 1.3.4, 2.2, 3.2, 4.1, 4.4, 5.1, 5.2, 5.3

Morris, M.R., Teevan, J., and Bush, S. (2008) Enhancing Collaborative Web Search with Personalization: Groupization, Smart Splitting, and Group Hit-Highlighting. *Proceedings of CSCW 2008*, 481-484. 2.2, 2.2, 2.3, 2.3, 3.1, 3.6, 4.1, 4.3, 4.1.1, 5.2

Morris, M.R., Fisher, D., and Wigdor, D. (2010a) Search on Surfaces: Exploring the Potential of Interactive Tabletops for Collaborative Search Tasks. *Information Processing and Management*, in press. DOI: 10.1016/j.ipm2009.10.004 4.2, 4.2, 4.15, 4.1

Morris, M.R., Lombardo, J., and Wigdor, D. (2010b) WeSearch: Supporting Collaborative Search and Sensemaking on a Tabletop Display. *Proceedings of CSCW 2010*, in press. DOI: 10.1016/j.ipm.2009.10.004 1.3.3, 2.1, 3.1, 3.2, 3.1, 4.2, 4.2.2, 4.20, 5.2

Morris, M.R., Teevan, J., and Panovich, K. (2010c) What Do People Ask Their Social Networks, and Why? A Survey Study of Status Message Q&A Behavior. 2.2, 2.2, 3.1, 3.3, 3.4, 5.1, 6.1, 6.1, 6.2, 6.2, 6.3

O'Conner, M., Cosley, D., Konstan, J., and Riedl, J. (2001) PolyLens: A Recommender System for Groups of Users. *Proceedings of ESCW 2001*, 199-218. 6.3

Paek, T., Agrawala, A., Basu, S., Drucker, S., Kristjansson, T., Logan, R., Toyoma, K., and Wilson, A. (2004) Toward Universal Mobile Interaction for Shared Displays. *Proceedings of CSCW 2004*, 266-269. DOI: 10.1145/312129.312230 4.2, 4.8

Paul, S. A. and Morris, M.R. (2009) CoSense: Enhancing Sensemaking for Collaborative Web Search. *Proceedings of CHI 2009*, 1771-1780. 1.3.4, 3.2, 3.7, 3.2, 5, 5.2, 5.2.1

Pawar, U., Pal., J., and Toyoma, K. (2006) Multiple Mice for Computers in Education in Developing Countries. *Proceedings of ICTD 2006*, 64-71. 4.2

Pickens, J., Golovchinsky, G., Shah, C., Qvarfordt, P. and Back, M. (2008) Algorithmic Mediation for Collaborative Exploratory Search. *Proceedings of SIGIR 2008*, 315-322. DOI: 10.1145/1518701.1518974 2.2, 2.1, 2.2, 2.3, 4.2, 5.2

Pirolli, P. (2009) An Elementary Social Information Foraging Model. *Proceedings of CHI 2009*, 605-614. DOI: 10.1109/ICTD.2006.301840 1.1

Raban, D. and Harper, F. (2008) Motivations for Answering Questions Online. In *New Media and Innovative Technologies*, 2008. DOI: 10.1145/1390334.1390389 1.3.5, 5.3, 6.2

Romano, N., Nunamaker, J., Roussinov, D., and Chen, H. (1999) Collaborative Information Retrieval Environment: Integration of Information Retrieval with Group Support Systems. *Proceedings of the Hawaii International Conference on System Sciences*, 1999. DOI: 10.1145/1518701.1518795 4.1, 4.2

Russell, D.M., Stefik, M.J., Pirolli, P., and Card, S.K. (1993) The Cost Structure of Sensemaking. *Proceedings of CHI 1993*, 269-276. 3.7

Schraefel, M.C., Zhu, Y., Modjeska, D., Wigdor, D., and Zhao, S. (2002) Hunter Gatherer: Interaction Support for the Creation and Management of Within-Web-Page Collections. *Proceedings of WWW 2002*, 172-181. DOI: 10.1109/HICSS.1999.772729 5.1

Shen, C., Lesh, N., Vernier, F., Forlines, C., and Frost, J. (2002) Building and Sharing Digital Group Histories. *Proceedings of CSCW 2002*, 324-333. DOI: 10.1145/169059.169209 4.2, 4.12

Smeaton, A.F., Lee, H., Foley, C., and McGivney, S. (2006) Collaborative Video Searching on a Tabletop. *Multimedia Systems Journal*, 12(4), 2006, 375-391 DOI: 10.1145/511446.511469 4.2, 4.11, 5.2

Smyth, B. (2007) A Community-Based Approach to Personalizing Web Search. *IEEE Computer*, 40(8), 2007, 42-50. DOI: 10.1145/616706.616710 2.2, 5.1, 6.3

Smyth, B., Briggs, P., Coyle, M., and O'Mahoney, M. (2009) Google Shared: A Case Study in Social Search. *Proceedings of UMAP 2009*. DOI: 10.1007/s00530-006-0064-7 1.1, 2.2, 4.1, 5.1

Stewart, J., Bederson, B., and Druin, A. (1999) Single Display Groupware: A Model for Co-present Collaboration. *Proceedings of CHI 1999*, 286-293. DOI: 10.1109/MC.2007.259 4.2

Sugiyama, K., Hatano, K. and Yoshikawa, M. (2004) Adaptive Web Search Based on User Profile Constructed without any Effort from Users. *Proceedings of WWW 2004*, 675-684. DOI: 10.1007/978-3-642-02247-0_27 6.3

Sun, J.-T., Zeng, H.-J., Liu, H., Lu, Y. and Chen, Z. (2005) CubeSVD: A Novel Approach to Personalized Web Search. *Proceedings of WWW 2005*, 382-390. DOI: 10.1145/302979.303064 6.3

Taylor, R.S. (1968) Question-Negotiation and Information-Seeking in Libraries. *College & Research Libraries*, 29(3), 1968, 178-194. DOI: 10.1145/988672.988764 2.1, 2.2, 4.1

Teevan, J., Alvarado, C., Ackerman, M., and Karger, D. (2004) The Perfect Search Engine is Not Enough: A Study of Orienteering Behavior in Directed Search. *Proceedings of CHI 2004*, 415-422. DOI: 10.1145/1060745.1060803 1, 3.2

Teevan, J., Dumais, S. T. and Horvitz, E. (2005) Personalizing Search via Automated Analysis of Interests and Activities. *Proceedings of SIGIR 2005*, 449-456. 2.2, 6.3

Teevan, J., Dumais, S., Liebling, D., and Hughes, R. (2009a) Changing How People View Changes on the Web. *Proceedings of UIST 2009*, 237-246. DOI: 10.1145/985692.985745 2.2, 5.1.1

Teevan, J., Morris, M.R., and Bush, S. (2009b) Discovering and Using Groups to Improve Personalized Search. *Proceedings of WSDM 2009*, 15-24. DOI: 10.1145/1498759.1498786 2.4, 2.2, 5.1, 6.1, 6.3

Tuddenham, P., Davies, I., and Robinson, P. (2009) WebSurface: An Interface for Co-located Collaborative Information Gathering. *Proceedings of Tabletop 2009*, 201-208. 4.2, 4.16, 5.2

Twidale, M., Nichols, D., and Paice, C. (1997) Browsing is a Collaborative Process. *Information Processing and Management*, 33(6), 1997, 761-783. DOI: 10.1145/1498759.1498786 2.1, 3.1, 3.2, 3.5

U.S. Department of Education, National Center for Education Statistics. (2006a) Internet Access in U.S. Public Schools and Classrooms: 1994 – 2005. 4.2

U.S. Department of Education, National Center for Education Statistics. (2006b) Public Libraries in the United States: Fiscal Year 2004. 4.2

Wells, A.T. and Rainie, L. (2008) The Internet as Social Ally. *First Monday*, 13(11), November 3, 2008. DOI: 10.1016/S0306-4573(97)00040-X

White, R., Kules, B., Drucker, S., and Schraefel, M.C. (2006) Supporting Exploratory Search: A Special Section of the Communications of the ACM. *Communications of the ACM*, 48(4), 2006. 1

White, R. and Roth, R. (2009) Exploratory Search: Beyond the Query-Response Paradigm. *Morgan & Claypool Series on Information Concepts, Retrieval, and Services*, 2009. 1

Wiltse, H., and Nichols, J. (2009) PlayByPlay: Collaborative Web Browsing for Desktop and Mobile Devices. *Proceedings of CHI 2009*, 1781-1790. 4.3, 4.24

Wittenburg, K., Das, D., Hill, W., and Stead, L. (1995) Group Asynchronous Browsing on the World Wide Web. *Proceedings of the Fourth World Wide Web Conference*, 1995. 4.1

Zhang, J., Ackerman, M., Adamic, L., and Nam, K. (2007) QuME: A Mechanism to Support Expertise Finding in Online Help-Seeking Communities. *Proceedings of UIST 2007*, 111-114. DOI: 10.2200/S00174ED1V01Y200901ICR003 5.3

Authors' Biographies

MEREDITH RINGEL MORRIS

Meredith Ringel Morris is a Researcher in the Adaptive Systems and Interaction Group at Microsoft Research. She is also an affiliate assistant professor of Computer Science and Engineering at the University of Washington. Merrie's main research areas are human-computer interaction and computer-supported cooperative work; her current research focus is on developing and evaluating systems that support collaborative Web search. Merrie was named a Technology Review TR35 2008 Young Innovator for her work on collaborative search. She has co-edited a special issue of Information Processing and Management on collaborative information seeking, and also co-organized multiple workshops on the topic. She earned her Sc.B. in Computer Science from Brown University and her M.S. and Ph.D. in Computer Science from Stanford University.

JAIME TEEVAN

Jaime Teevan is a Researcher in the Context, Learning, and User Experience for Search (CLUES) group at Microsoft Research. Her research centers on how our digital past can help shape our future. Jaime was named a Technology Review TR35 2009 Young Innovator for her work on personalized search. She co-edited (with William Jones) the first book on Personal Information Management, co-edited a special issue of Communications of the ACM on the topic, and organized workshops on PIM and query log analysis. Jaime has published more than 30 technical papers, including several best papers, and received a Ph.D. and S.M. from MIT and a B.S. in Computer Science from Yale University.